changing
the message

JEFF ALBIN

A HANDBOOK FOR EXPERIENTIAL PREVENTION

Published by:

Wood 'N' Barnes Publishing & Distribution
2717 NW 50th
Oklahoma City, OK 73112
(405) 942-6812

Cover Design by Blue Design
Copyediting, Interior Design & Layout by Ramona Cunningham

Printed in the United States of America
Oklahoma City, Oklahoma
ISBN # 1-885473-58-3

To order copies of this book, please call:
Jean Barnes Books/Creative Solutions
405-946-0621 • 800-678-0621
www.creativesolutionscatalog.com

Dedicated to Mom,
who believed in me when I did not believe in myself
and inspired me when she broke her arm
while riding her mountain bike at the young age of 62.

 # ACKNOWLEDGEMENTS

This work is far from complete. That may be a strange thing to say at the beginning of a book, but I realized as I began writing that there will be many more ideas and activities to come. I will consider my work to be complete when the schools where I've worked implement this model without my help.

So many people have helped shape my thinking that I cannot remember them all. When the people I work with found out I was getting published, they all wanted to know 1) if they would get a free and/or autographed copy and 2) if they would get mentioned in the acknowledgements. Just so nobody gets left out, if I have worked in your classroom, I am in your debt—but you still have to buy a book.

With all that said, I would like to acknowledge pivotal people who have profoundly influenced the twists and turns I've chosen to take, and I will do it in the spirit of Jack Kerouac (e.g. the endless sentence): Connie Bender for sending me to my first ACOA meeting; Buck Ghosthorse for putting me in my first sweatlodge and reintroducing me to my spiritual ways; the "guy" who belayed me so many summers ago at YMCA camp; Mary Jean Poirier and Doug McComas; Sam Fast Buffalo Horse for teaching me compassion; the entire Ghosthorse Tiospaye; Sundancers everywhere past and present; the countless youth who have taught me more than I will ever teach them; Karl Rohnke, "the godfather" of experiential education whom I still have not met; Laurie Frank for the inspiration her book *The Caring Classroom* provided; my wife Vicky just for having to live with me and my weird ideas; my supervisor Sandy Mathewsen for believing in me and always backing me up; authors Peter Senge and Alfie Kohn, whom I also hope to meet someday; the teachers who have allowed me into their classrooms; my family, who provided so many hours of valuable issues to learn from; Jared Zeff for teaching me about the true nature of disease; and of course Michael Becker, who is going to build a better world one organic radish at a time.

There are two teachings that stick with me. The first of these is the power of the circle. Visualize all of these names and many more standing in a circle and building a better world. The second teaching is to "keep the peace." This was the message of a man named Deganiwida. They called him the "Peace Maker." He created the Haudoshanee league a long time ago. It is his vision that I follow today, one classroom at a time.

PUBLISHER'S NOTE

We live in a crazy world, and maybe we always have. Sometimes to keep the pace, we create realities to cope with the dysfunction. When we create these realities they are frequently unhealthy. With these mixed signals we send others the wrong message of how to live correctly in our world.

Our goal is to help people deliver a different, healthy message—a message full of possibility, resilience and hope. Jeff's living narrative and creative facilitation of the powerful lessons included in this book will inspire us all to "change the message."

We would like for this book to bring some new energy, focus, and challenge to the current "prevention" models. We're all headed in the same direction with the goal of creating healthy humans. We think Jeff's got the right idea: skip the talking heads, or at least augment them, and "meet the group, where they're at."

Jeff's been at this for a long time. He's an experienced facilitator and has learned his safety rules one student at a time. We encourage you to heed his words of caution on activities that may be a little more involved, challenging, or physically or emotionally demanding. The cautions we have "built-in" to the text are meant to prompt activity facilitators to use their noggins and to make the safety of the participants their primary focus. We encourage you to experience the activities yourself before presenting them to your audience, and involve trained, certified instructors, designers, and builders if the task is beyond your training or expertise.

We join Jeff in issuing the Ultimate Challenge (page 113) to those of you who share his heart and vision of sending out a new message and creating a new world one student at a time.

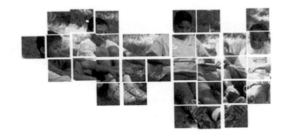

Any given activity can be done just for fun (and some days that is as important as anything), but the real value lies in the weaving together of the activities and lessons, and in the building of trust and open communication.

FOREWORD

I had only been at Lyle School a couple of weeks when one of the other teachers in the middle school told me that the "drug and alcohol guy" would be around that week and from what he had seen of me so far he thought we might get along well. From what I knew about most "drug and alcohol guys," I was not sure if this was a compliment! I come from a background of Outdoor School, science camps, Outward Bound programs, and life as a climbing bum, so I was not really into the standard classroom experience, and I was certainly not looking for someone else to bring it into my room. My ADD brain was not looking forward to sitting through those movies about what your lungs look like after smoking either. For a long time, I have believed that students need scenarios that allow them to experience the process of making decisions and facing consequences (in a somewhat controlled atmosphere) so that when exposed to real-life problems they have a solid level of experience to draw upon. The structure and supervisory role is to ensure we don't head off to "The Lord of the Flies" but also not to micromanage the decision-making process to the point that the experience has no real value or impact on the student.

I was in the field outside my classroom door debriefing an initiative activity with my class when I first met Jeff Albin. He just stood and watched as we wrapped up our discussion.

"What are you doing here?" Jeff asked. I answered something about my efforts to build more of a sense of community within my class.

"How does that fit into your curriculum?" was his next question. I replied that I really didn't know where it fit into the "curriculum," but that to me it was a crucial piece and more important than any particular lesson or curriculum. I told him I felt that until we could function as a group, our chances of being much of a class were pretty low.

Ever since that moment, Jeff Albin and his ideas have been a fundamental part of the learning community I have strived to create here at school. Little did I know what an asset the "drug and alcohol guy" would become in facilitating a classroom climate that I had theorized for years. His wisdom, creativity, and absolutely wacky sense of humor endear him to the kids. More important is the impact on kids when his ideas and methods begin to challenge them to function differently in his absence. They begin to approach tasks, problems, and free time in a different, more playful way.

The ideas and activities in this book ask people to take on a higher level of responsibility for themselves. Any given activity can be done just for fun (and some days that is as important as anything), but the real value lies in the weaving together of the activities and lessons, and in the building of trust and open communication. The facilitator has the role of linking the experiences in the activities to the rest of the world in a way students can relate to. This book is a valuable tool in offering that link. These types of activities have often been done in short, intense workshop or group dynamic sessions. The model that Jeff advocates is that all students should have access to these types of activities repeatedly over the course of their education. That by developing inquisitive, critical thinkers who have experienced many problem-solving situations and processed their solutions, we will see groups of kids that make better decisions. Students with a history of this process remember old strategies and increase their creativity, thinking up new solutions. The old model of "fix the bad kids" not only does not work, but it arrives too late. The model of choice here is wellness for all, with abundant and positive choices and outcomes as a part of the process of development.

It may sound as if there is too much expectation and requirement of experience on you as a facilitator. But that is the real beauty of these ideas: The only true requirement is that you begin. Somewhere, anywhere! Find a simple activity that feels like something you can pull off and give it a try. Even if it is a total flop, your group will have an experience to talk about. Don't be afraid to be a part of the circle of learners that any group really is. Some of the greatest flubs I have ever seen turned out to be some of the most profound experiences. From the beginning you will get many ideas about your group and yourself that will steer you to the next experience. Pick a time to do the next activity and let the group know so they can look forward to it, or cancel a math quiz and play Smackdown. Don't be in a hurry for dramatic results and changes; long-term cultural change takes time if it is going to last. As the group progresses, let the students become the facilitators, inventing their own games and activities and also processing their own experiences. Don't wait; there are all kinds of trainings you can attend later, and they will be better if you have a little experience under your belt. Pick an activity and GO PLAY!

Michael Becker, M.Ed.
8th Grade Teacher
Lyle School
December/2003

CONTENTS

COMMENTS FROM SOME OF JEFF'S KIDS:

What I like about the bandana game is that it was fun and a really awesome game. –Brenda, 4th grade

Thank you for all the things you have done with us. It was fun. I especially enjoyed being outside and not sitting at my desk. –Vanessa, 4th grade

We all got pretty silly and started laughing. –Caleb, 4th grade

Oh, have I told you thank you for playing all those games with us? –Lisha, 4th grade

I liked how we took turns listening to other peoples' ideas. –Sam, 4th grade

You helped us here. At the ropes course, you are why I went on the giant swing the second time. You got others to do things like butt wrestling, and that takes time to build up. You helped a lot here, so thanks. –Ian, 8th grade

You taught us how to have a positive attitude on matters. And you allowed us to be able to speak up about matters. And you came up with games that allowed us to relieve our stress without ending up with detention or a bloody nose. –Jennifer, 8th grade

Thanks for coming here so often and doing stuff with us. I know it might not seem like it, but it really helps. –Hannah, 8th grade

You have taught us the skills that math and science couldn't (I'm not saying they aren't important) but they can't teach us to trust, put up with each other or problem solve how to get ten people up in a tree. –Michelle, 8th grade

I just wanted you to know that I've learned a lot from you. And because of the things you do with us I know I feel more comfortable doing things with my classmates and I get along with them better. –Doug, 8th grade

I remember key experiences from my youth that brought me to where I am now. Snapshots of experience.

INTRODUCTION

It's hard to tell where a train of thought starts. All I can do is point out highlights along my journey of understanding. I might call them snapshots of experience. I remember key experiences from my youth that brought me to where I am now. When I was about 12 years old, I went to YMCA camp. In 1973, ropes courses were beginning to pop up everywhere. As part of its ropes course, the camp had a giant rope swing. To get on this thrill ride, I climbed a 20-foot tower unassisted and unbelayed. (Challenge course safety standards have changed a lot since then.) Then I sat on a little piece of plywood attached to a rope and swung to the stars. Another part of the course was a rappelling wall. An instructor on the ground wrapped me in a webbing pretzel known as a Swiss seat. I climbed to the top and rappelled down. Other experiences I recall from that camp include starting a fire without matches and a long backpacking trip.

By the time I was 16, I was heading down two roads. I was heavily involved in drugs and alcohol, and I was spending most of my free time outdoors. Around this time, I was approached by the director of a youth program who was starting an outdoor club. He wanted me to teach orienteering to 6th graders. This was the beginning of a long guiding career. Looking back now, I can visualize what happened. A group of concerned adults was sitting in a room talking about "at-risk youth." My name most assuredly came up, and somebody thought it would be good to put me in a leadership position. By the time I was 18, winter breaks were spent in snow camps with my friends. My best friend was a trapper, and all of my friends hunted.

I was leading sea kayaking, rafting, and back-country skiing trips both for an outdoor club and professionally when I started college. College to me was out of classes by noon and on the water or the mountain by one o'clock. My senior project in science class was "Applied Physics, Hydrodynamics on Class Five White Water."

In the summer of 1984, I soloed the Inside Passage from Washington to Alaska. I would have graduated that fall were it not for a chance meeting with an orca whale. It was early dawn. The mist was still heavy, and I was utterly alone in my kayak a few miles from the town of Butedale, British Columbia; population: three. I heard what sounded like a gunshot 50 yards behind me. It was a male orca breaching and slamming the water. A few seconds later he was right in front of me, and then he was gone. I said to myself, "Man, I've got to find a way to get summers off." That fall I enrolled in the Western Washington University School of Education and spent two years there getting an education degree and a secondary teaching certificate.

Fast forward: I have quit drinking. I spent two years working in an inpatient psychiatric treatment unit (PTU) for adolescents. It was an end-of-the-road place. The jails would send our kids back because they could not handle them. Within those two years, I became the supervisor of the person I had originally been hired to assist. I saw firsthand the effects of abuse and addiction on youth. Although all of the kids had an official diagnosis, every single kid was from an alcoholic family. I decided at that time to become a chemical dependency counselor.

Around the time that I left the PTU, I met a Lakota man named Buck Ghosthorse. That story is several chapters in itself, but the relevance for this curriculum is his vast knowledge of traditional family structures and how they can be a healing and stabilizing force. I was adopted by his family, and my experiences around that are constantly shaping and reshaping my notions of family and community.

After working in several treatment centers and running a sea kayaking business, I ended up in Goldendale, Washington. Several things happened around that time that led to the model I am presently using. I started working as an Intervention and Prevention Specialist for ESD 112. My job was to get kids into treatment, assist them in their recovery and provide prevention services.

I also met a man named Jared Zeff. He was an internationally known naturopath. He taught me about immune systems of the body and how they could be strengthened through individualized diet, exercise and other techniques.

I combined Zeff's knowledge of disease, Lakota family thought, Alfie Kohn's views on education, Claudia Black and John Bradshaw's work on family systems, Peter Senge's work on organizational development, experiential learning, what worked for me as a kid, and my experiences working with alcoholics and addicts into an intervention model that I have come to call "Experiential Prevention." There have been quite a few other influences, but that is a pretty long sentence. Most people call people like me "eclectic," which I think is a nice word for scattered. I do, however, want to mention *The Caring Classroom* by Laurie Frank (recently updated and expanded as *Journey Toward the Caring Classroom*). It's the best curriculum I've ever read mainly because I agree with everything Laurie says.

A thumbnail sketch of Experiential Prevention looks like this:

1) Disease Theory of Alcoholism

   a) Primary: It is a primary diagnosis. It does not happen because of another diagnosis.

b) Chronic: It does not go away. It can only go into remission.

c) Progressive: If untreated, it will only get worse.

There are two primary approaches to disease.

1) Allopathic: This is the approach most people are familiar with. It is heavily dependent on drugs and surgery. It is rarely preventive in nature, although that is changing. A primary approach of this model is to look at disease as an outside, invading force. The doctor's job with his arsenal of technology and pills is to stop the invaders in their tracks. The patient is often a bystander in the process.

2) Naturopathic: This approach looks at disease as an imbalance within the system. It is very preventative in nature. Naturopaths focus heavily on strengthening the immune system. The patient actively participates in his own healing and wellness. The naturopathic approach is much slower, and patients unfamiliar with this approach may become impatient. A fundamental principle is that the solution lies within the problem.

My experiences in life and work have led me to choose, whenever possible, the naturopathic approach. The disorder of any individual within a system is merely a magnification of the disorders present in all individuals in that system (Kohn 1998). Until we treat the entire system we will only be measuring percentage points. When the system is healthy and the immune system is strong, disease cannot survive.

This book is not just an activity manual, nor is it intended to be an articulation of big theories. I do encourage you, however, to explore the authors I have mentioned. The primary purpose of this manual, much like experiential learning, is to open a door. The structures that support it should be familiar to the users of this guide. Additionally, the purpose of this curriculum is not to divulge my personal life story, but my background is an important part of the foundation.

I have heard it said on more than one occasion that challenge or ropes course activities are an oral tradition. We tend to use the activities that we have experienced ourselves. I use many activities that are not in this manual. They must be experienced. If you intend to use this approach, I highly urge you to receive training.

CHANGINGMESSAGE

FACILITATOR'S TOOL BOX

We teach what we need to know.
We take our teach and teach him slow.

f you are anything like me, you will skip the introduction and this toolbox section and jump straight to the activities. If that works, great! If not, you may want to refer back to the instructions (aka the facilitator's tool box). Like any good American male, I prefer to try to put the "some assembly required" toys together without reading the instructions. It gives me more play time. Sometimes, though, like the time I wired my 110-volt battery charger to my 220-volt plug on my generator, getting more information would have been helpful.

It was the first winter in our solar-powered, off-the-grid house. The previous owners had just unplugged everything whenever they went through long periods without sun. We decided we did not want to live in a completely rustic fashion, so I ordered a rather expensive 75-amp battery charger. Eager to get back to civilized living, I rushed home and wired it in. I turned my generator on and went to our back porch. An ethereal blue smoke drifted slowly out of the top of my brand new battery charger. I quickly unplugged everything and said a silent prayer of thanks that my house had not burned. After another week and a "kaching!" with the credit card, I had yet another new battery charger. This time I had an electrician friend help me wire it in.

The number-one rule of doctors is "First do no harm." Counselors, teachers, facilitators, and anybody who works with youth should follow that guideline. Although low and high ropes activities are just plain fun, there are tools you do not want to be without when you begin. Venturing into trust activities before your group is ready is a prime example.

I often tell people, "Ropes is the medium, not the message." The message is healthy schools, healthy classrooms, healthy families, and healthy communities. I weave in a healthy dose of Disease Theory of Alcoholism, Family Roles, and now Media Literacy. I stay away from extensive information on particular drugs when I am doing prevention. I consider that to be intervention. As with any guideline, however, the needs of your school may change. If your kids are doing a lot of huffing, quite clearly some education is needed.

I have been working with two ideas in the past year that seem to make sense. The first is **sustainable wellness**. Sustainability is a popular buzzword now. An increasing number of people are looking at the price of excessive materialism and realizing that it cannot continue. I stole the concept of sustainability and applied it to wellness. Much of the initial, well-intended prevention work of the past focused on scare tactics and information absorption. An often-quoted statistic is that 450,000 people die from smoking every year. That's sad, horrible, and even criminal. It has little impact, however, when a kid who feels he has no future and really has no understanding of death hears that if he smokes, someday he's going to die. Sustainable wellness is a holistic approach. Look at the school environment. How do those fluorescent lights affect learning? If a kid is eats Doritos® and drinks Mountain Dew® for breakfast, can he be expected to focus on algebra? What if a kid is terrified to come to school because he knows he will be bullied? A focus of any prevention program should be to reduce disease-causing factors (sugar for breakfast) and increase the immune/protective factors. To move toward sustainable wellness, everything that affects the system must be scrutinized.

You may not get rid of the pop machines this year, but don't give up. Remember the story of the quantum pond. I'll give you the short version:

> *There was a man who walked by a pond every day on his way to work. Each day that he passed that pond, he would throw a stone into it, hoping to make a ripple. Every stone he threw, however, failed to create even a splash. This went on for years. It puzzled the man, but he continued to throw those stones. One day a young boy passed the pond and threw a stone into it. Suddenly, a huge wave arose from the pond. Delighted, the boy bodysurfed all day long. The End*

The second concept is **contextual counseling**. Professional counseling has only been around for a little over a hundred years. The model of counseling still popular in schools and communities is what I call the deficit model. You take the troubled youths (aka the Bart Simpsons), ship them to a remote corner of the building, and try to fix them. Meanwhile, the system that created them does not change. Contextual counseling is a systemic approach. When I am doing ropes activities in the classroom day in and day out, I have the opportunity to deal with behaviors and attitudes as they occur. I hear from quite a few intervention and prevention specialists that they have trouble getting kids out of class. The solution? Get into the classroom! I'll end this with a quote I saw on a T-shirt: "It's easier to build a boy than to mend a man."

FACILITATE (DON'T TEACH)

Even the blind squirrel gets an acorn every now and then. —Michael Becker

I have an enormous concern that sometime somewhere somebody will pick up my curriculum, follow it precisely, and find it an absolute failure. Anybody who has worked with me for any length of time has discovered that my program is highly effective but that the plan can be changed rapidly. That is the nature of facilitation.

It was March, 2003. For many people in education this is the longest month of the year. Students traditionally become more restless, there are no government holidays, and spring break is everybody's focus. March is the metaphor. I tell students that if our process can survive March, it can survive anything.

I arrived in the 7th-grade classroom with my trusty lesson plan and my bag o' tricks. As I walked into the room, it became clear there was trouble in paradise. Somebody had put gum in somebody's hair. Lines were drawn, and people were digging in. It looked as if all of our previous group development work was about to be torpedoed. The teacher and I convened a talking circle, but that didn't work. In fact, it seemed to make the problem worse. Hmmmm, they didn't cover this in counselor school.

I came in the next day with a video—a skull-crushing, boredom video on neurobiology. Unlike other days, we didn't circle the desks. The students stayed in straight lines. They obediently watched the video, but they were giving me quizzical looks. I had never shown them a video. Mr. Becker, who had been primed for this, sat behind his desk. After the video was over, I told the class that this was the first in a series of twelve educational videos. I thanked them for trying my new approach to drug and alcohol education and expressed my regret that it wasn't working. I explained that I would be going back to a more traditional approach because that would probably work better. I thanked Mr. Becker for letting me try the new ideas and told him I would be back Monday with the next video in the series. With a straight face, he thanked me and said he would reserve some time on Monday. I made certain that I did not show anger or displeasure. I was quite clinical, actually. With the students sitting in stunned silence, I left the room.

Mr. Becker told me later that after I left, the classroom looked like a beehive that had just been tipped over. The students immediately went into action. They spent nearly two hours processing. They talked through some serious issues. They agreed to work on some issues and let others go. Mr. Becker just sat behind his desk and continued playing his role. Finally, they sent an emissary to my office. They showed me their new Full Value Contract and asked if I would reconsider doing the activities instead of showing the videos. We went on from there. I call this "consciously invoking the paradox." Using paradox is not something I would recommend for new facilitators. It worked for me because experience had shown me when and how to use it.

Another magic moment from this last school year occurred on the Giant's Ladder at the high ropes course in the Klickitat gym. The Giant's Ladder is a series of horizontal 4 x 4 beams connected with stainless steel cable. The task is to climb to the top, and it's usually done with a partner. The person climbing is always being belayed from the ground. Two 6th-grade boys started climbing together. One boy quickly became frustrated and came down. The second boy continued to climb. Each beam was a struggle. His classmates began, without any prompting to focus intently on his efforts. He came to the second-to-the-last beam. One more and he would be to the top. By this time, however, he was quite fatigued. He made multiple attempts to get to that last beam. When he was still and contemplating his next effort, the class sat in hushed anticipation. When he tried to climb, they were hooting and hollering encouragement. His teacher had tears running down her cheeks. He spent nearly an hour trying. Finally, because school was over, we brought him down. Words will never do justice to the magic of that hour.

Facilitation is helping people to get where they need to go. Different people have different needs. A "recipe card" approach to experiential prevention is to be avoided. My first activities with any group are diagnostic. I watch how they do what they do. I notice where their process works and where it needs some help. I focus on strengths and stay in the positive. After that, activities become prescriptive. They are chosen and designed to meet the needs of the group. I could have easily lectured the 7th-grade class or put the clamps down. The lessons they gained could never have been planned. I also could have pulled that boy off the Giant's Ladder in order to make sure more people got a turn. Somehow "turns" were not as important that day.

SPONTANEITY IS WHEN YOU DEVIATE FROM YOUR PLAN

I need to know that quickly. I need to be able to shift directions so smoothly that nobody knows it's not just part of the plan.

Snow never lies. After a fresh snow, I wander through the woods around my home and see what the residents have been up to. From quite a distance away, I can tell whether the tracks are a coyote or a deer. Coyotes never walk in a straight line. They sniff here, urinate there. They are insatiably curious. They are so curious that they will stare at a rancher long enough to be shot. Deer, on the other hand, walk in straight lines or gently curving lines. Mostly they are shy. They often bolt as soon as you see them. Young deer, however, will eventually turn around and look to see what's following them. Ravens, the wise jokers of the forest, are almost impossible to stalk. They harass me, laugh at me, and joke in large groups about the pitiful human in the forest below.

Human beings never lie either. They always leave a trail for you to follow. Some part of them cannot completely conceal what's going on with them. Sometimes it's a look. Sometimes it's body posture. As a facilitator, I need to know who left the tracks, what the tracks mean, and how I can use the information. The same is true when working with groups. If I start down the trail of group development and nobody is willing to follow, I'm just wasting my time. If I do an activity the group is not ready for, I need to recognize that quickly. I need to be able to shift directions so smoothly that nobody knows it's not just a part of the plan.

A time-honored method for a quick evaluation of any group is the GRABBS (Goals, Readiness, Affect, Behavior, Body, Stage) modality. This was first articulated by Schoel, Prouty, and Radcliffe (1988) in the adventure education classic *Islands of Healing*.

GOALS: Does the chosen activity match the goals of the group? A poorly chosen activity will only lead to unnecessary frustration.

READINESS: Does the chosen activity match the stage of group development at which your team is functioning?

AFFECT: What do the facial expressions of your group tell you? Are they bored? Are they excited?

BEHAVIOR: What behaviors are you seeing? Are they drifting away? Are they focused?

BODIES: What are their bodies telling you?

STAGE: Are they storming? Are you still doing icebreakers when you could be doing complex initiative problems?

ALWAYS OVERPLAN

An adventure facilitator cannot be toting around stacks of books or curriculums full of activities. Get some sticky pads. Know shorthand or make up your own. When I plan for a group of people, whether it's a group of teachers or a kindergarten class, I plan enough activities so there is no danger of running out of things to do. I write it all down on my sticky pad and put it in my shirt pocket. After the session is over, I write down everything that group has done (see the Activity Log on page 124).

BE A FUN PERSON!

That's fun, not phony. A lot of people want to know what my secret is, as if there were some formula to follow. I want to know too. I have some vague ideas. I have had some lengthy conversations with other successful facilitators about why some people can do this stuff and others can't. Michael Becker, 8th grade teacher at Lyle Middle School, told me that to make it work, you pretty much had to have been a knuckle head back in your own school days. That's true for me, but I don't know if it's true for others. What I know about people who are successful with kids is that they are **real**. What you see is what you get. They have a great sense of humor about everything—especially themselves. In the schools where I work, I am known as a "good-time Charlie." When I show up, kids expect to have fun, be challenged, and learn something they didn't know before. Kids remember the stuff they learned because of two main factors. First, they're moving. They generate a kinesthetic body memory. Second, they have fun. People tend to remember times when they were laughing.

DO YOUR OWN WORK

"You can't teach what you don't know" is an often-repeated belief statement that may or may not be true. I prefer to rephrase it to "Don't take people to places where you are not willing to go yourself." The true nature of experiential group development is that you know you're going on a journey, but you don't truly know where you will end up. The intensity will be different for different people. You may have your trusty curriculum in hand and be ready to start at the cooperation or forming stage, but your group may already be at performing and ready for high-level trust activities.

If you are doing ATOD (alcohol, tobacco, and other drug) and violence prevention, you need to be very clear on where you are with your own issues. If you are a recovering alcoholic or a child of an alcoholic, you need to understand clearly that "NOT EVERYBODY COMES FROM A DYSFUNCTIONAL FAMILY!" Since I am always asking people to grow and change, I make sure that I am always growing and changing.

An unwritten rule for anybody who works with children has always been not to discuss disagreements in front of the children. This is often true, but we need to understand that every skill a child learns he learns by seeing an adult do it first. It's important that kids see adults disagreeing in healthy and functional ways and still working together with respect.

FIDELITY TO THE PROGRAM

WHAT? That's right. This is a program, a curriculum, a model. It is time-tested and successful. It would be more accurate to say, however, that facilitators should have fidelity to the principles and structures that are the foundation for adventure programming. The activities themselves will vary widely between facilitators. Often, I make them up on the spot or design them to meet a particular need.

The first structure concerns the stages of group development. The model I use is adapted from Scholtes (1988). Scholtes placed norming before storming. Perhaps because I am working in the school system, that simply has not been my experience. We seem to move right from forming to storming. The norms emerge from the storm just like flowers after the flood.

FORMING

Forming starts when the group gathers for the first time. They check each other out. They explore boundaries. They want to know what is acceptable and what is not. They may have anxieties about making sure they have a "spot." Discussions are around surface issues. Situations are discussed from a "problem" stance. Safety is a primary concern, although it may not be articulated.

STORMING

This is where the teacher's eyebrows will raise almost to the hairline. Arguing and defensiveness are common. Putdowns may be heard. Group members will express impatience with the process. People with control issues will be louder and more boisterous. Introverts may fade and disappear. People may choose sides or reinforce existing divisions. It looks like the group will fall apart. Teachers who have been taught to maintain control of their classroom will wonder where this is all going and may try to reestablish control.

NORMING

At this stage the group looks more functional. If there is criticism it is constructive and informational. The group will naturally move toward cooperation. Group members will share deeper levels of personal information. A sense of belonging is common. Members have a firm understanding of their roles as well as their strengths and weaknesses. There is a higher level of commitment.

PERFORMING

Groups at this stage have developed a process for approaching any task. All members are listened to and respected during discussions. Each member is seen as valuable. Members recognize when the process breaks down and can self-correct. Members are loyal to each other. Individuals listen intently to constructive feedback.

Other thinkers have added two more stages to this model:

TRANSFORMING

A highly functioning group can develop the capacity to bring about life-altering changes in the lives of its individual members. They may choose healthier habits, break free from unhealthy relationships, or work for changes in the larger community. Anything is possible. A good example of this is the social activism many members of Alcoholics Anonymous practice when it comes to policies around alcohol, tobacco, and other drugs.

ADJOURNING

At some point the process needs closure. The school year is a natural conclusion. I remind my groups that how we say good-bye is just as important as how we say hello. There is often a mad rush to get to the end. It is quite easy to lose hard-gained ground.

EXPERIENTIAL LEARNING CYCLE

The second structure with which you need to be entirely familiar is the "Experiential Learning Cycle" (Kolb 1984).

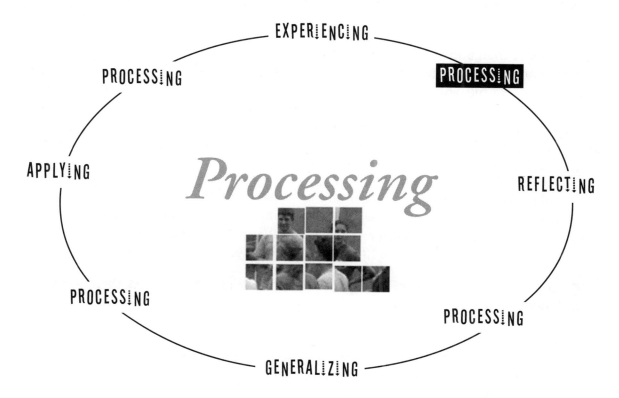

You will notice that processing occurs continually. In my own skewed version of reality, the Experiential Learning Cycle has been around a lot longer than 1984. A couple million years ago, a few of my ancestors were clustered around an unknown plant. The conversation went something like this:

"Do you think it's edible?"

"Somebody needs to try it."

Org tries the plant. Org (a) drops dead or (b) lives and even loses a few unnecessary pounds. The tribe, or rather Org, has had an experience. He reflects, "Hm, tasted good." He generalizes. Maybe eating too much of the plant could be a bad thing. What if he kept losing weight indefinitely? Maybe he could just eat it sporadically. Org will apply his new knowledge. He will continue to experience, reflect, generalize, and apply.

Having a working knowledge of this model will help you immensely in your understanding of how to facilitate experiential prevention activities. The experience alone is not always enough for kids or even adults to integrate the lessons. A quality debrief must be a part of each session or training.

DEBRIEFING

There we were, once again rescuing defeat from the jaws of victory. —Sam Dunlap

Perception tells us more about the mind of the perceiver than the object being perceived.
—Buddha

Debriefing and then applying the lessons to everyday life is what helps people grow. If, however, you do a 20- to 30-minute experiential activity and follow it up with a 45-minute discussion every time, you may lose your audience. Some groups, however, can process at length. In one consensus lesson with a group of 4th-graders, they chose to spend nearly four hours discussing the issue. That, however, is highly unusual. The activities are simple to follow and create. Quality debriefing is a skill acquired over a lifetime. For beginning facilitators I recommend the following:

1) Go online to a company called Training Wheels®. It has many tools for processing. My favorite is the "Body Parts Bag." Kids love it too. It has a small foam rubber heart, eye, feet, brain, guts, and a smiley face. Natural questions or prompters accompany each body part. For the eye it's "Tell me something you saw."

2) Copy the following questions onto some 3 x 5 cards and then stick them in your back pocket. It's a little wooden, but it's a good start.

TRUST
What did it feel like to have the entire group supporting you?
What needs to happen for us to build trust?
How have we built trust?
Did we do anything to erode trust?
Who is the person you trust the most?
What qualities make that person trustworthy?
What qualities do you share with that person?

COMMUNICATION
Was our communication effective or ineffective?
Did we respect different opinions?
Was everybody listened to?

GROUP DECISIONS
Did a person's perceived status influence the decision process?
Were you okay with how decisions were made?
What is the best way for us to make decisions as a group?

LEADERSHIP AND FOLLOWING
Who became the leader in this activity?
How do we choose leaders in this class/school?

What are the qualities of a good leader?
Is the leader the one with all of the good ideas?
Do leaders ever get tired of being leaders?
Does anybody who is usually a follower want to be a leader?

FEEDBACK
Did you give feedback to somebody today?
Did they listen to you?
What sort of feedback works for you?
Did you give feedback in a way that they could take it in?

COOPERATION
Tell me about a time when you saw the group cooperating.
How does it feel when we cooperate?

PROBLEM SOLVING
Did you make a plan?
Did everybody know the plan?
How was this problem similar to or different from other problems?

3) Roger Greenaway from the UK has a free Web site devoted entirely to debriefing. The address is http://reviewing.co.uk. If that address doesn't get you there, type "active reviewing" into a Google® search to find him.

4) Get a set of Chiji® cards. Go to Chiji.com. If you don't have money for that, make your own debriefing cards from clip art or magazine clippings.

5) For new facilitators, try the **DATA** model.
    a) Describe what happened.
    b) Analyze what happened.
    c) Transfer what you learned.
    d) Apply what you learned to real life.

6) Discuss issues "in the round."
    - The high point for me was ...
    - The low point for me was ...
    - The hardest thing for me was ...
    - The easiest thing for me was ...
    - What surprised me was ...
    - Something I knew would happen was ...
    - Nobody listened when ...
    - My motivation went down when ...
    - My motivation went up when ...
    - I was helped by ...
    - I helped ...
    - I appreciated ...
    - I'm really pleased that I ...
    - I wish I had ...
    - I felt like going home when ...
    - If I'd had a camera ...
    - If I could do it again I would ...
    - I wish I had been asked ...
    - I was annoyed when ...
    - I was appreciated by ...
    - I'd like to complain to ...
    - I'd like to congratulate ...
    - I'd like the group to tell me ...
    - One last thing I'd like to say is ...

People may not listen well if they are too anxious about what they will say for their turn. This pressure can be reduced by:

- Allowing time for thinking or making notes before a round starts.
- Allowing passing, or repetition of what someone else has said.
- Starting with different people for each round.

Rounds can be overused with the result that the routine stifles discussion rather than stimulates it—so mix rounds with more free-flowing methods.

7) Debriefing Bingo (from *Teamwork and Teamplay* by Jim Cain): After reflecting on the experiences, be prepared to discuss the following events by choosing a line of five boxes in a row. For example, you can discuss five separate events during today's experience in which you may have: listened to someone (Tell about it), tried something new (What was this new thing?), considered a different point of view (Share it with the group), played outside your comfort zone (What event put you there?), and offered someone encouragement (Who were they?).

Laughed	Changed Something	Offered a Suggestion	Developed a New Skill	Listened to Someone
Used My Problem-Solving Skills	Said "Thank You"	Was Glad to be Part of This Team	Tried Something New	Assisted Someone
Saw Something Amazing	Cheered	Considered a Different Point of View	Made an Improvement	Sacrificed Personal Goals for the Good of the Group
Tried, But Just Couldn't Do It	Played Outside of My Comfort Zone	Applauded	Learned Something New	Expanded My Personal Boundaries
Offered Someone Encouragement	Played a Different Role	Considered a Different Point of View	Felt Challenged	Asked Someone for Help

8) Talking Circle: Once a week, once a month, or whenever necessary, convene a talking circle. The rules are simple. One person talks at a time, and it goes in a circle. Be very strict about those two rules. The circle does not work without them. It's good to have an object that belongs exclusively to the class—a stick, a stuffed animal or whatever the class chooses. When I do this with adults, I use either my grandfather's compass from WWI or a stick that was gifted to me by an eagle dancer at a Sundance. This object can be passed around the group, and only the person holding the object can speak. Center initial questions around what's working, what's not working, and highlights from the week. As time moves on, questions can go to a much deeper level.

If you look at most models for debriefing, you will notice that they have an application segment. I continually ask kids to make small changes. It can be as simple as eating lunch with somebody they haven't eaten with before. After a discussion with a group of 3rd-graders about how bad it felt to be excluded, they all committed to practice inclusion at recess by making sure that everybody who wanted to play was allowed.

MEET 'EM WHERE THEY'RE AT

Sam Dunlap, a range manager for the Forest Service had a large sandbox for a desk. Ranchers, many of them illiterate and therefore unable to read a map, would come into his office and arrange the dirt and other small props to reflect their understanding of the landscape. In this way, Sam was able to clearly understand where the ranchers were keeping their cows. These "men who draw in the dirt" had a great respect for Sam because they knew he respected them.

A crucial part of ropes activities is sequencing. I sometimes hear the comment from teachers, "We've tried that teambuilding stuff before. It doesn't work here." If you follow the recipe-card approach, you may experience disaster. If you do "trust" because trust is on the schedule today and your group is not ready, it will be worse than if you had done nothing at all. A typically successful sequence looks like this:

1) Icebreakers
2) Cooperation Activities
3) Trust Activities
4) Challenge Activities/Initiative Problems
5) High Ropes Course (if available)

Notice how this sequence parallels the stages of group development. The time between #1 and #3 may be an afternoon or three months. "Meet 'em where they're at!"

CONSTRUCTIVISM

The field of constructivism deserves a book in itself. What is handier is a checklist of guiding principles.

1) Everybody is a learner who is actively seeking and constructing new meanings.
2) Mistakes help us learn and are valuable in and of themselves.
3) People learn best from people they trust.
4) People learn best from experiences in which they are passionately interested and actively involved.
5) Goals can change rapidly as learners acquire new information and new skills.
6) Learners must incorporate new information into past experiences in order to give that information meaning.
7) Teaching (facilitating) is the process of providing learners with experiences, activities, and prompts that enable them to create meaning through self-regulation.
8) The best predictor of what and how someone will learn is what they already know.

A COMMON AGREEMENT

Think about ham and eggs. The chicken is involved, but the pig is fully committed. –unknown

A common agreement is an integral part of experiential prevention. It is a negotiated agreement between all members. When kids come up with rules, they are more likely to follow them. I emphasize, however, that if I am to work with them, certain items are non-negotiable. Putdowns are not allowed, and physical safety is always paramount.

Another constant component is "Challenge by Choice," developed by Project Adventure®, a leading organization in the field of experiential education.

> *The concept of Challenge by Choice allows each person to be in control of his/her level of participation. It means that a person may choose what s/he wishes to share with the group about him/herself. It means that a person may choose to be totally involved physically and emotionally in an activity, or choose to sit back and watch. It does not mean that a person sits and reads the newspaper while the group goes about its business. No matter what level of participation an individual chooses, s/he is still part of the group, even if it means being an observer (Frank, 2000).*

When misused it becomes "Challenge by Shame." Reframes of this concept are "Choose your trust" and "Choose your own level of involvement."

Some optional models and helpful ideas:

a) Portable Hand Model:
   Pinky—Physical and emotional safety.

Ring Finger—Commitment to the process, working toward individual and group goals.
Middle Finger—Respect.
Pointer Finger—Direction, goals, a reason for doing what you're doing.
Thumb—Feedback. In order to integrate the lessons, kids need time to process. Giving feedback is a vital part of this process.

b) Basic Model (good for getting started):
Play Hard
Play Safe
Play Fair
Nobody Gets Hurt

c) Family Model:
This one is simple. I ask the class to brainstorm a list of rules of healthy families. I write them all down on a sheet of butcher paper. If everybody agrees and the list looks reasonable, then you have a common agreement. (See Qualities of Healthy Families on page 123.)

d) Good Friend Model:
Ask your kids to brainstorm a list of the qualities that make a good friend. That list becomes your rules.

e) A Common Being:
You will need a sheet of butcher paper long enough for the tallest class member to lie down on. One at a time, each class member lies down on the paper and part of their body is traced by another class member. When it is done, you will have traced a part of each person's body. The end product is a combination of the entire class. It usually gets some laughs. (Often discomfort will be expressed when you get to the crotch area. My experience has been that females are generally okay tracing females wearing pants.) Inside the outline, have the class write down qualities they value. Outside the outline, they should write things they want to avoid. Typically words on the inside might be words like "respect" and "trust." On the outside, the class will hopefully come up with words like "putdowns" and "dishonesty." Sometimes they need prompting with words like "inclusion."

CHANGING MESSAGE

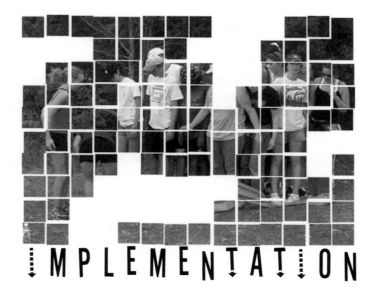

IMPLEMENTATION

hope by this time you have an idea of what experiential prevention looks like. How you implement it is an issue for you to discuss with your staff. I have the luxury of working in small, rural schools where the entire 9th-grade class might be 15 kids. When I first started in my present position, I was working in seven schools in 5 days. This hectic schedule forced me to do a program that would quickly grab the class's attention. Low Ropes was a natural option. I just reframed everything to meet prevention goals. For about 6 years, I kept that crazy schedule. My program worked, but not nearly to my satisfaction. When the Professional Development Plan came in the mail from "cubicle land," my gears started rolling.

I looked at my options and decided to ask my boss if I could adjust my schedule. Rather than being in a school every Monday of every week, I wanted to try being in a school for a month at a time and see what would happen. I also found what I think is the best book ever written in this field. The book is *The Caring Classroom* by Laurie Frank (recently updated and expanded as *Journey Toward the Caring Classroom*). Laurie's book reinforced my beliefs about the next step in what I had been doing in the schools. It's a book that every person who works in schools should have on his/her shelf. Implementation of my experiential prevention model has met with rave reviews. In one school, I am allowed into every classroom from kindergarten to 12th grade for an hour each day except Fridays. I had to reserve Fridays for interventions in the schools where I would not be working that month.

The success of the program has varied with the teachers whom I am working with. One teacher is also a ropes course facilitator. I can leave him with the theme of the debrief and know that he has the ability to follow through on it all day or even all week long. That's when the model really starts to blossom, and the survey numbers reflected that difference. An interesting phenomenon in that particular classroom has been the reinforcement of the "myth of the outside expert." Although that teacher has a very similar background to mine, he does not always get the same results from similar activities. This is mainly because he's with them all day long. When we co-facilitate, it's a powerful combination.

If you accept my theory that this program is a way to build the immune systems (aka resiliency) of your students, it follows logically that you have to look at dosage. How often do you need to do these activities in order to achieve the desired outcomes? Certain personality types can do these activities all day long. Others, often introverts, quickly tire of intensive group interactions. You also have to consider what you want your outcomes to be. If you want to eliminate bullying in a school where that is the norm, you may have to go slowly. This type of program tends to promote equality. If the power brokers are unwilling to yield their positions, the pace may be slow.

When I do presentations to teachers and counselors at in-services or conferences, I am often asked how I deal with resistance. I have a single response: "I Don't." That is to say, I don't engage in resistance. Implicit in this approach is choice. During the school day, students have few choices about where, when, and how to be in the world. When their behavior gets out of control, the hammer comes down in the form of some archaic approach to discipline such as suspension. They have few opportunities to learn self-management. In one class of juniors and seniors who had not been exposed to experiential learning of any sort, a student asked me why I never gave them the solutions to the problems I presented. I responded by saying that philosophically I felt like I would be cheating them if I just gave them the answers. She accepted the answer but was still clearly puzzled. I rarely encounter resistance. With one class, students somehow received the message before I arrived that I was there to fix them. The deficit thinkers had arrived ahead of me. I informed the class that they were free to not participate. Within a week, they were back. The critical element in that situation was that I gave them a choice.

> When resistance happens, I move with the energy. If I force this program on students, I have defeated myself and stolen their freedom. Remember: community, not coercion.

Certain situations, however, can present teachable moments. When I worked as a crisis worker on an alcohol and drug help line, I often ended up at the jail in the wee hours of the morning talking to late-stage alcoholics. I would ask them, "Well, how's life working out so far?" In the same way, if a class is experiencing a lot of friction and the accompanying detention, suspension, and other penalties, I will ask them if they like the way things are.

The big hook of experiential prevention is that it's fun. Kids are moving, exploring, running, thinking. I have cool props like rubber chickens, webbing, and mousetraps. The activities engage them on multiple levels.

Some schools implement this type of programming into their PE programs. It's a natural fit because many of these activities are active, but some PE teachers may need training in debriefing. I worked with several PE classes this year. The only complaint I received was that I was leaving to work in the next school.

Cross-age teaching should be a long-term goal of any experiential prevention program. It fits the needs of healthy schools on multiple levels. Older students integrate the lessons they've been learning by teaching them to younger students. Younger students listen better to the students they look up to. It frees up teachers who are already maxed out by the demands of education reform. If all those reasons still haven't convinced you, the price is right. High school students work for free during the school day.

Gaining access to some classrooms can be problematic. One teacher promised full access but always seemed to need to do something else when the time came. Experiential prevention can look suspiciously like fun, and that can be a threat to the more traditional educators. Just as with any other group of people, I meet the teachers where they are. At some point, the class will ask, "How come we don't get to do activities with Jeff?" When the door opens, I enter.

GOALS OF EXPERIENTIAL PREVENTION

The goal of any experiential prevention program should be to assist all students in developing their capacity to make healthy and informed decisions about all aspects of their lives. We want to help children develop a broad range of problem-solving and critical thinking skills that can be applied to any situation in their lives. In a classroom that functions within the model I have developed, each student has several people he can turn to in times of difficulty. Students can give and receive feedback in ways that benefit themselves and their fellow students.

The recent data regarding the alarming rise in juvenile diabetes and obesity indicates that we need a more holistic health focus when it comes to prevention. Remember that the goal of experiential programming is to raise the overall immunity level and therefore the resistance/resiliency of each child. When the community is healthy, the children are healthy. When a child begins to use ATOD, that represents an imbalance in the overall health of the system of both the child and the community.

> *That an entire society shares the same pathology*
> *does not make that society sane.* –Erich Fromm

When I was in early recovery, I was astounded by the poor health of people who were otherwise "clean and sober." As I watched one man suck down an alarming amount of coffee, cigarettes, and the ubiquitous donuts available at AA meetings, I felt compelled to ask him, "Aren't you concerned about your health now that you're sober?"

He gave me a sideways glance and said, "When you have as much sobriety as me, then maybe you'll understand."

"Boy, I sure hope not." That brought a welcome close to the conversation.

PREVENTION PRINCIPLES FROM N I D A

Prevention programs should be designed to enhance protective factors and move toward reversing or reducing known risk factors.

Prevention programs for adolescents should include interactive methods, such as peer discussion groups rather than didactic teaching techniques alone.

Prevention programs should be long term, over the school year with repeat interventions to reinforce the original prevention goals.

Family-focused prevention efforts have a greater impact than strategies that focus on parents only or children only.

Community programs need to strengthen norms against drug use in all drug abuse prevention settings, including the family, the school, and the community.

Prevention programs should be adapted to address the specific nature of the drug abuse problem in the local community.

The higher the level of risk of the target population, the more intensive the prevention effort must be and the earlier it must begin.

Prevention programs should be age-specific, developmentally appropriate, and culturally sensitive.

Prevention programs should include skills to resist drugs when offered, strengthen personal commitments against drug use, and increase social competency (e.g., in communications, peer relationships, self-efficacy, and assertiveness) in conjunction with reinforcement of attitudes against drug use.

Prevention programs should include a parent's or caregiver's involvement to reinforce what the children are learning—such as facts about drugs and their harmful effects—and to open opportunities for family discussions about use of legal and illegal substances and family policies about their use.

So that's the official stuff from the feds. It's a good list of principles, but just like the man medicating himself with nicotine/sugar/caffeine, it doesn't go far enough for me. In any given population only 10 to 15 percent of the people will develop chemical dependency. Children need skills to deal with the curveballs that life throws—divorce, death, trauma, economic dislocation, and bullying, among other issues.

For quite a few years, I taught wilderness survival skills. Instead of focusing my classes on just the rudimentary skills of matchless fires, shelter, and food procurement, I worked with participants on strengthening their minds and bodies so they could feel confident in any environment. It's no different with experiential prevention. The mind is the tool we need to sharpen. When we give away our minds to anything, whether it's drugs, sex, gambling, video games, or abusive partners, then we become slaves. "Addict" comes from the Greek word "addis," which means slave.

As you go through this handbook, you will notice that not all of the activities are framed with ATOD messages. If I framed every activity that way, I would quickly lose my audience. All of the activities are, however, framed with the overall goal of classroom health. Happy programming!

No man is an island, but many are large peninsulas.
—Michael Becker

ICE BREAKERS

If you are anything like me, you have skipped straight to this section. Happy hunting.

Most people naturally put up barriers for protection. Kids in small-town schools may have known each other for years and have huge issues with each other. Kids in other schools will cluster together in "cliques." One time I was asked to do a half-day teambuilding session with a group of teachers. We negotiated a common agreement in the classroom. As we got ready to move to the gymnasium, I asked them to "leave any baggage in this room." Under her breath, one teacher said, "I don't think this room's going to be big enough." As a facilitator, your first job is to "break the ice." At some point you will want to introduce the concept of "comfort zone." It often looks like this:

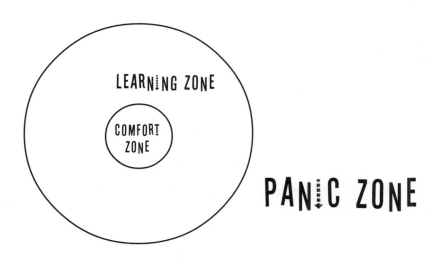

Beyond the learning zone lies the panic zone, and beyond that what the Japanese call *satori* or enlightenment. Another way to look at the comfort zone is to reverse the circles. The panic zone becomes the inner circle. Looking inside at ourselves can be a scary experience. Enough deep stuff. Here are some surefire games to "break the ice."

> UNFAMILIAR ENVIRONMENT
> + UNFAMILIAR SITUATION
> ──────────────────────
> NEW STRATEGIES & NEW SOLUTIONS

ICE BREAKERS

 ## BANDANA TAG

NEEDS: At least two bandanas for each participant. I have a bunch of bandanas because I get them off the giveaway blankets after our ceremonies. You can get cheap bandanas at the dollar store or make your own from fabric remnants.

PROCEDURE: Have the participants tuck (not tie) their bandanas into each side of their waistbands. Hanging onto the bandanas with their hands and physical contact are not allowed. The goal is to steal everybody else's bandanas while trying to avoid losing yours. If they lose their bandanas they can quit, take a rest, or try to steal somebody else's. Any stolen bandanas are tucked into the waistband. If a participant has no way to tuck in the bandanas, provide a piece of webbing to tie around his waist or borrow a belt from the flag football equipment.

FACILITATOR NOTE: This has been a top seller. Kids enjoy it because they can participate at their own level of involvement.

 ## CLOTHESPIN TAG

NEEDS: Give each participant four clothespins. Where would adventure programming be without the dollar store? I can usually get 72 wooden pins for $1. Don't get the plastic pins. They never last. You will also need a rubber chicken and a Hula Hoop®.

PROCEDURE: Start with the group in one area and place the rubber chicken in the Hula Hoop® some 40 yards away. The object of the game is to be the first to clip all of your pins on the clothing of the other participants. After doing so, run and grab the chicken and jump up and down while shouting, " I won, I won, I won!"

VARIATIONS: Participants steal clothespins that are already clipped onto people's clothing.

OBSERVATIONS/QUESTIONS:
Follow up with a short discussion on the nature of competition.
When is cooperation helpful, and when is competition helpful?

After about two weeks of doing exclusively cooperative, everybody-wins-type games with a class of 3rd-graders, they told me they didn't like the competitive version and came up with a never-ending game similar to bandana tag.

 ## METAMORPHOSIS TAG

PROCEDURE: Everybody starts as an egg. The order goes like this: egg, chicken, dinosaur, cheerleader. To advance you must play Rock/Paper/Scissors with someone who is at the same stage you are. When an egg beats an egg, the winner becomes a chicken and continues on up the ladder. The goal is to become a cheerleader. Cheerleaders stand off to the side and cheer on the process. I usually do this for about three rounds.

OBSERVATIONS/QUESTIONS: This game was first introduced to me as Evolution Tag. In the small, conservative, rural communities in which I work, the word "evolution" can be a "hot" word. Last time I checked, I was not a science teacher. It's not my job to debate stuff like evolution. I'm the fun guy, and you are too. Remember?

 ## MAD MAX

PROCEDURE: Mad Max is Simon as in "Simon Says." I usually demonstrate each scenario. With younger groups, I will introduce just two scenarios initially. Once they master those, I introduce more.

1) Tubing: Two people lay on the ground to form the inner tube. The third person is the "tuber."
2) Speedtrap: One person sits on the ground with his head in his hands. Another person is the officer writing the ticket.
3) Fish On: One person is the fish. One person is catching the fish. Four other people are fishermen who haven't caught any fish all day.
4) Rockslide: Eight people form an avalanche of rocks by making their bodies into little balls. One person is the driver of the car.

Every time a person is left out of one of these combinations, or forms one without first saying "Mad Max Says!" s/he has to go to Fisher Canyon and chant, "Two boats enter, one boat leaves!" (It might help to watch Mad Max in *Beyond Thunderdome* before you lead this game.)

Example: Facilitator says "Tubing." Participants scurry into position. Facilitator says, "I didn't say 'Mad Max says.' You all have to go to Fisher Canyon and chant 'Two boats enter, one boat leaves.'"

Facilitator says "Mad Max says 'Fish on.'" Participants scurry into position.

FACILITATOR NOTE: I generally avoid elimination games unless they are frivolous in nature. Mad Max and similar games are active mixers. To stay in the game, participants must join forces with those whom they might not choose otherwise. It focuses on the ever-important skills of listening and watching. This is the Klickitat Canyon version. You can easily adapt the situations to meet your local circumstances.

I generally don't debrief this unless something obvious needs to be addressed.

 ## SALMON/BEAR/MOSQUITO

NEEDS: Rope or webbing for a dividing line and some kind of boundary markers, such as cones, bases, or rope. Gymnasiums have plenty of convenient lines.

PROCEDURE: Split the group in half in some creative fashion. One half of the group is on one side of a line (rope or webbing) and the other half is on the other. Salmon/Bear/Mosquito is a variation of Rock/Paper/Scissors:

> Bear Eats Salmon
> Salmon Eats Mosquito
> Mosquito Eats Bear

Have each group practice their animals. Bears hold their hands up and roar. Mosquitos make a stinger with their pointer finger, put that hand pointing out from their nose (not in) and make annoying nasal mosquito sounds. Salmon are silent with both hands at chest level palm to palm, and they have to make fish lips. If you don't know how to make fish lips, imagine you just sucked a lemon or ask any 3rd grader.

At some distance from the center line on both sides (20 to 40 yards) place the boundary markers. This is "base" or the safe zone. Once people are on base they can't be tagged.

Send each group to its "base" to huddle up and decide which animal to be. After making their decisions, they all stand about 3 feet back from the center line. On the count of three all group members must imitate their chosen animal. If their animal eats the other group's animal, they run and try to tag the other team members. Anybody tagged becomes part of the team that tagged them. If their animal is an "eatee," they must try to make it safely back to their base. Huddle up and do it again.

OBSERVATIONS/QUESTIONS: This is a game in which players shift sides frequently. Although most tag games need little debriefing, this game can be a good opportunity to talk about the difference between cooperation and competition. Occasionally a player will face the entire group all by his lonesome. You may hear, "That's not fair." When this happens, I take that teachable moment and have a brief discussion about "fair." To many people, especially kids, "fair" means that everybody gets the same thing. At this point, I introduce the concept that "fair" can mean that everybody gets what they need. To illustrate this, I point out that the needs of an infant are quite different from the needs of a full-grown adult.

FACILITATOR NOTE: An easy way to divide the group in half is to have them choose in their minds one of two opposites (e.g., fire and water, winter and summer). This is probably a good time to mention that it's always a really bad idea to have "captains" choose team members. Remember getting picked last for something back in junior high and how yucky that felt?

LOOK FOR OTHER CREATIVE WAYS TO DIVIDE YOUR GROUP IN THE "BRANCHING OFF" SECTION ON PAGE 36.

 VROOM

NEEDS: A long (at least 50-foot) piece of 1-inch tubular webbing or retired climbing rope with the ends tied together.

FACILITATOR NOTE: I use a double barrel knot for rope and a water knot for webbing. I like the double barrel knot because it allows me to quickly adjust the diameter of my ropes. Water knots for webbing are simple and easy to remember (for directions, see Teaching Tools and Resources).

PROCEDURE: Have everybody stand in a circle with both hands on the rope. Their first task is to pass the knot around the circle quickly. You can build enthusiasm by having the group make race car sounds as it's going around—hence the name. Introduce the other sounds and corresponding actions as you go along.

   Vroom sounds: knot goes left
   Brake sounds (errrrrrrr): knot stops
   Train sounds (chuga chuga chuga): knot goes right
   Airplane sounds: hands go up in the air
   Submarine sounds (dive, dive, dive): hands go forward, down, toward the center

FACILITATOR NOTE: Make sure nobody gets rope burn. This is a good time to talk about the importance of safety. If everybody's safe, it's time to move on.

OBSERVATIONS/QUESTIONS: I've done this game with people from ages 4 to 63. It may work with people over 63. With kindergartners you may have to watch to make sure they don't pile on top of each other.

CAUGHT YA PEEKIN'

PROCEDURE: This one's simple. The group stands in a circle. Everybody closes their eyes. The object is to catch somebody else peeking. If you see somebody peeking before they see you, say their name, point at them, and say "Caught ya peekin'." It's competitive but only in a silly way.

ZIP-BANG

PROCEDURE: Another simple one. The group stands in a circle. Start the group off by saying "Zip" or "Bang" to the person next to you. "Zip" goes left. "Bang" goes right. The only catch is that you can't show your teeth. Once you show your teeth, you're out. Direction can change at any time.

VARIATIONS: Another version of this is "Snort." Making your best and grossest pig sound, you snort to either your left or right. If the person you're snorting at laughs, they're out.

SMACKDOWN

NEEDS: Each person gets a foam noodle. Noodles or foam bats can be found at most toy stores in the spring and summer. I usually cut the 6-footers in half. For purchasing information, see Teaching Tools and Resources.

PROCEDURE: The rules are simple. If you're holding a noodle, you are agreeing to play. People may hit you with their noodles. If you drop your noodle, nobody can hit you. If you pick your noodle up again, you are back in the game. Keep rounds from 3 to 5 minutes each.

FACILITATOR NOTE: Head shots are illegal and will result in a player being removed from the game. I also tell the class that ganging up is forbidden. Every now and then, exuberant players will go 2 to 1.

OBSERVATIONS/QUESTIONS: This is another game that allows all players to choose their own level of involvement. It is a great ice breaker and energy mover, but I always frontload it with a conversation that starts with the question:

"What's the difference between violence and aggression?"

Depending on your audience, you will get a lot of responses. It serves as a quick needs assessment. After the conversation has gone as far as it can go, I introduce this definition:

"Violence is aggression without somebody else's permission."

Using sports as an example, I tell the group that in football if a person is not aggressive he will probably sit on the bench. I then go on to further define violence as putdowns, taking things without permission, maliciously gossipping, etc. This is a good time to talk about how people want to be treated in the classroom.

Ninety-nine percent of the time I will hear: "Treat people like you want to be treated."

In a gentle way, I point out the fallacy of this statement. If I treat everybody like I want to be treated, I am assuming they are like me and I am not being fair. I reframe this as: "Treat people like they want to be treated."

SPROUTBALL

NEEDS: A lot of "throwables." In my bag of tricks, I have 4-inch fleeceballs, which are available in most PE catalogs. I also have a dozen or so similarly sized stuffed sheep which I found right before Easter at the dollar store in Yakima. A good throwable does not hurt upon impact but can be felt when it hits you. It can also be lobbed a considerable distance with some degree of accuracy. Fleeceballs are great, but something about throwing stuffed sheep around seems to loosen up most audiences.

PROCEDURE: Everybody gets two or three throwables. The object is to run around and throw your fleeceball or sheep at the other players. When you are hit, you are frozen. When the player that hit you gets hit, you are back in play.

FACILITATOR NOTE: Again, head shots are illegal and will result in a player being removed from the game. I also tell the class that ganging up is forbidden.

ASTEROIDS/SHEEPAROIDS

NEEDS: Throwables. See Sproutball for more information.

PROCEDURE: No, "sheeparoids" is not a word, but it sure sounds funny. Remember these are ice breakers. This game is quite similar to Sproutball. Everybody gets two or three throwables. The object is to run around and throw your fleeceball or sheep at the other players (head shots are illegal, ganging up is forbidden). When you are hit, you are frozen. In this game, however, you can reenter the play as soon as a ball that is in play comes within reach.

VARIATIONS: To demonstrate the difference between cooperation and competition, try this: Start out the same, but when you're hit, you're out and you have to stand by the wall.

Standing by the wall seems to emphasize the "losing" aspect. Last one playing wins. Do this two or three times, and then introduce the game with the above rules. Usually you will find that most kids prefer the cooperative version of sheeparoids.

 RUBBER CHICKEN TAG

NEEDS: A rubber chicken or an acceptable substitute.

PROCEDURE: You need a small and well-defined area for this game. The person who is "it" puts the rubber chicken between his knees and hops around trying to tag someone. The person he tags then becomes "it." This game is highly aerobic and generally doesn't last more than 5 minutes a round.

OBSERVATIONS/QUESTIONS: This game does not always work with middle schoolers because the chicken often takes on a new meaning. This is a good game to introduce after you have worked with your class for a while.

 "HELP ME" TAG

NEEDS: I have several rubber chickens in different states of decomposition. I also have a rubber pig which came with my original portable ropes courses. I use most of them in this game.

PROCEDURE: I tell the kids that I grew up on a farm, and in the wee hours or when everybody was away, the animals would play together. The pigs would chase the chickens all night long in an endless game of tag. This has nothing to do with the rules of this game, but it helps loosen up my audience.

The person holding the pig is "it." If a person is holding a rubber chicken she cannot be tagged. To get the rubber chicken, the person being chased must say, "Help, I need the rubber chicken!" Then the person holding the chicken should pass it to the person calling for help. I start with just one rubber chicken and add more if necessary. Emphasize that a person cannot get the chicken unless he asks for it.

OBSERVATIONS/QUESTIONS: I watch my group closely during this activity. A "performing" class will hardly ever allow the pig to catch the chicken. A couple of good debriefing questions after this would be:

How is our class at asking for help when we need it?
Is this something we can improve on?
Do I ask for help when I need it?

ENERGY TOSS

PROCEDURE: Once your crowd of middle schoolers is standing quietly at attention in a circle explain these simple rules.

- They are to toss an invisible energy ball which can change size, velocity, and any other characteristics quickly. Each person should keep his/her eyes on the other participants' eyes to "see" where the ball goes.

- No one can hold the ball longer than three seconds or s/he is out of the game.

As the circle shrinks, the energy seems to intensify. That's what I've experienced. After your circle shrinks to just a few screaming loonies, start over and introduce another rule.

- This time when the energy ball comes to a person, the people on the other side of the circle must help catch and throw it. If they don't or if they are caught unaware, they must step out.

OBSERVATIONS/QUESTIONS: This deceptively simple activity has the potential to bring out the wildest side of your extroverts. It may not be a great opener with the wrong crowd. Poorly timed ice breakers can actually make more ice.

I generally don't play "elimination" games, but in these type of situations it doesn't seem to adversely affect the class dynamics. The introverts can quietly retire, and the extroverts can tightrope on the edge.

SAVE THE CHICKEN

NEEDS: A spot marker for each participant. A rubber chicken, foam boat, or bandana (with younger children, I use a bandana).

PROCEDURE: Have the group form a circle, and have each participant stand on a spot marker (only one person to a spot marker). Start with a person in the center of the circle, standing on a spot, holding the chicken. The person in the center uses the chicken to tag any person standing in the circle, quickly returns the chicken to the spot marker, and tries to get back to the taggee's spot before getting tagged by the taggee. Get all that?

After it looks like your students have that part down, introduce a new rule. Any person can move to any open spot. This makes the game move pretty fast.

When it seems like they have that pattern down, try this last rule. When the chicken is sitting on the center spot, any person can take a risk by rushing forward, touching the chicken, and saying, "Save the chicken, save the chicken!"

OBSERVATIONS/QUESTIONS: When the game really gets going, you may choose to "freeze frame" and remind your students about safety. Credit Erik Marter from Synergo with this one.

 BALLOON SYMPHONY

NEEDS: Enough large balloons for each participant to have one.

PROCEDURE: Divide participants into six to eight groups. Give one balloon to each person. The task is to play a song using only balloons. The other groups must guess the song. Weird, huh? This one came from Erik Marter from Synergo, too.

 GROSS

NEEDS: A bag of lint.

PROCEDURE: The 3rd-graders were seated in a circle on the carpeted floor. After the obligatory shuffling and "be quiet you guys" to each other, they focused in. I put on my serious face (probably not a sustainable practice) and showed them the bag. "In this bag is something that is very important to my family. It's something that the men in my family have passed down from generation to generation for hundreds of years. Close your eyes, pass the bag around, and see if you can guess what's inside."

They solemnly passed it around. Several guesses were made. Nobody could figure it out, not even the teacher. "This is a bag of belly button lint from all the men in my family!"

"Gross!!" (accompanied by laughter)

OBSERVATIONS/QUESTIONS: In the writing of this book, I have been reflecting on why I use humor when dealing with alcohol, tobacco, and drug addiction. I want people to know that there is incredible joy in my life. I want kids to see that being without alcohol, tobacco, and other drugs is fun, because it is. My disease of alcoholism has been my greatest gift. I find humor in many things, especially myself. Institutional wisdom and bureaucratic logic make easy targets. Of course, one hazard of being a trickster is that I sometimes trick myself. In keeping with my life principles, that's when I laugh the loudest. When I teach people about conflict, one of the first rules I try to teach them is to be the first one to find humor in the situation. It will most likely be funny later, so why not laugh now instead of later?

BUTT WRESTLING

PROCEDURE: Grab your ankles. The whole point of the activity is to either make your opponent lose his grip on his ankles or knock him over. When you are deep into this activity, your principal will show up...guaranteed.

OBSERVATIONS/QUESTIONS: This has been a great hit with the middle school boys, but few of the girls have displayed an interest. In middle school, body issues have to be considered constantly. Any accidental references to body parts or functions can quickly defocus your audience. As any seasoned middle school teacher can tell you, you just have to roll with it.

 BATTLESHIP 1

NEEDS: Enough webbing circles for half the class.

PROCEDURE: 1) Divide into pairs.
2) Each pair gets a webbing loop.
3) One person with each pair issues a challenge to a person in another pair.
4) The partners must agree upon their choice of Rock/Paper/Scissors.
5) The person that "loses" joins the other team. She can either be a "captive," staying on the inside of the loop and having no voice in the decisions, or join as a full member.

FACILITATOR NOTE: Bryn Dawson's kindergartners were walking around holding onto webbing loops in groups of two's and three's while playing Rock/Paper/Scissors. Bryn is committed to making her classroom a warm and welcoming environment. She uses elements of the TRIBES program and is attentive to her students' needs that fall outside of the regular curriculum. She was intrigued by the activity. "What is this teaching them?" she asked.

"I'm not sure," I replied. "I just thought of it coming down the canyon. It seems to work pretty good though, doesn't it?" She agreed.

A goal of much of this curriculum is to broaden the horizons of my participants. A way to do this in their immediate environment is to ask them to work and play with people with whom they would not ordinarily interact. This can be accomplished by directly telling or asking them. A better way is to play.

OBSERVATIONS/QUESTIONS: Although it was purely chance, some interesting things happened. One team captured quite a few and their loop became unwieldy. Some of the "captives" spontaneously joined the team. It was easier to join, they told me later. I've tried this with quite a few age groups. I don't debrief it a whole lot, but it is certainly rich with metaphors about "winning" and "losing."

BATTLESHIP 2

NEEDS: Enough webbing loops and foam bats for half the class.

PROCEDURE: This game resembles Battleship 1 in that you begin by dividing the group into pairs and each pair holds onto a webbing circle. Give one person in each pair a foam bat. One at a time, teams challenge other teams to a duel. The first person to strike a blow captures the other dueler. The captive can either stay inside the loop and remain a captive or join by holding onto the outside of the circle. The captive gives the bat to the remaining team member, or if a team captures the last person with a bat and a webbing loop, they get to use those items. When a team has captured four loops, four bats, and the people that come with them, that team becomes a "battleship." There is no logic to the number four or the title of this game. It's just what popped into my head at the time. If you have ever played blob tag, this will look familiar.

FACILITATOR NOTE: Head shots are illegal. I don't use foam bats with students younger than 11 or 12. With middle school students, the bats are a great way to teach boundaries. If somebody plays too roughly, they just don't play.

VARIATIONS: Appoint a "Navy SEAL" or a whale with a different colored hoop. The SEAL/whale team does not play by the same dueling rule. It can capture anybody at will. This can lead to great discussions about "fair."

 ## HUNKER HAWSER

NEEDS: Two sturdy, plastic buckets and 50 feet of 1/2-inch rope. I use retired climbing ropes. Avoid sisal or manila ropes as they can cause rope burns.

PROCEDURE: The game is pretty simple. Two people stand on sturdy plastic buckets about 8 feet apart playing a game that resembles tug of war. Each person is holding one end of the 50-foot rope. The goal is to make the other person step off her bucket or drop her end of the rope.

FACILITATOR NOTE: Participants need to be advised that it may be necessary to step off the bucket in order to avoid falling. Have spotters ready behind the people on the buckets. I caution them before beginning that falling is likely.

OBSERVATIONS/QUESTIONS: When I was teaching this game to a class of 9th-graders it suddenly occurred to me that I had been playing this game longer than any of them had been alive. Talk about your reality checks! Scott Teitelbaum taught this game to us while we waited for the shuttle bus on the Deschutes River. It's called Hunker Hawser because you have to hunker down to win and *hawser* is the German word for rope. I hope life has treated you well, Scott.

Although I use this mostly as a transition game, I have had some interesting discussions about what the game has to do with human relationships. This is another game that allows all players to choose their own level of involvement.

 ## TOE TAG

PROCEDURE: Have partners place their hands on each other's shoulders. Challenge them to tag the toes of their partners (using their toes) before their partners tag their toes. This looked pretty Irish to me for some reason.

 FINGER TAG

PROCEDURE: Have partners clasp each other's hands (as if they are preparing to arm wrestle) with their index finger extended. Now have them try to tag each other using their index finger. Play until one player makes five tags.

 BITE THE BAG

NEEDS: A paper grocery bag.

PROCEDURE: Have the group form a circle. Set the grocery bag in the center of the circle. The challenge is to stand on one foot and "bite the bag." No hands are allowed. After everybody that wants to try has tried, fold the top of the bag down about an inch. Keep folding the bag down until only a few people can bite the bag.

OBSERVATIONS/QUESTIONS: I learned this game in 1984 on the same river trip where I learned Hunker Hawser. While this is an elimination game, I have experienced watching people who may not shine in other areas succeed at this. It's important to provide a variety of activities so that all the kids have a chance to show their stuff.

 I WANT TO KNOW SOMEBODY WHO...

NEEDS: Dots or spot markers for each player.

PROCEDURE: This game has been around a long time. Have the group form a circle with everybody standing on a dot. One person stands in the center. She says "I want to know somebody who has on blue jeans (was born in Oregon, etc.)." Whatever she says must apply to her. Everybody else to whom this applies has to move at least three spaces away. When there is only one person left, he moves to the center and it all starts again.

VARIATIONS: At a recent Northwest Association for Challenge Course Technology conference I learned the partner version. The game is the same except that you are linked with a partner. What you say has to apply to both of you. When you move, the statement also has to apply to both of you. It's a subtle way to learn common ground and to emphasize the importance of thinking about other people.

BRANCHING OFF

Back when I was dabbling in organizational development, I ran into a book called *Orbiting the Giant Hairball*. It was written by Gordon MacKenzie, a man who managed the quirkier part of Hallmark®. He cautioned against using terms like "division" when dealing with organizations. Since then, I have tried to pay attention to the power of language. I prefer "branching off" to "dividing" into pairs or groups.

PAIRING UP

- Distribute dominoes and instruct each person to match one end of his/her domino to another person's domino.

- Put each child's name on a popsicle stick and place them in a can. Draw two at a time like a raffle.

- Cut pictures from magazines or old greeting cards in half. Have participants find the other half of their picture.

- Have half the group remove their shoes and toss them into the center of the circle. The other half crawls with their eyes closed and picks a shoe. They open their eyes and find their partner. Yes, smell can be a hazard.

- When I have been working with a group for a while and they are familiar with my principles, I will ask them to pick the last person they would pick if they were going to pick partners. This works for me, but be sure your group is ready before you do it. How will you know when they are ready? Ask them?

TO DIVIDE A LARGER GROUP: A simple and quick technique is to have participants silently pick one of two (or more, depending on the number of groups you need) similar things. They must keep their choice to themselves until asked to branch out.

Coffee or Tea
River or Mountain
Shoe or Sock
Table or Chair
Potato or Tomato

Truck, Car, or Van
Blue, Red, or Green
Sunny, Rainy, or Foggy
Basketball, Football, or Baseball
Frog, Toad, Lizard, or Snake

For a "Boomer" crowd (self-identified by knowing the term "Boomer"), have them choose their favorite Beatle:

John: The Rebel and Revolutionary
Paul: The Traditionalist

Ringo: The Mascot
George: The Mystic

THE POTATO SPROUTS METHOD

Create four circles of chairs in the room. In the middle of the first circle, place a conventional looking Mr. or Mrs. Potato Head®. In the center of the second circle, put an unconventional version with ears where mouths ought to be, all arms, or feet on top of the head. Use your imagination. In the third circle, place a real, raw potato. In the fourth circle, place a fairly conventional Mr. or Mrs. Potato Head® with some minor deviations such as two mouths or three ears.

If you ask your class members to choose one of the circles, they will likely just follow their friends. To ensure integrity, have them write down the spud they've chosen on a piece of paper and fold the paper in half. An interesting discussion can result when you ask students to explain their choices.

LONGER-TERM BRANCHES

While a lot of activities can be done with large classes, students tend to share more freely when their "learning branch" is fifteen or less. In one classroom we invested an hour in creating these branches by using Yin/Yang processing cards, Pocket Processors, which I had recently purchased from Chiji®.

Each card has opposing statements on it such as "keep my thoughts to myself/share my thoughts openly" or "always stick to the rules/follow the rules when they make sense." I had the class move along an imaginary continuum, with those who agreed with one statement on one side of the continuum and those who agreed with the opposing statement on the other side of the continuum. To keep the students moving, I kept switching the topics on the cards. When the introverts and extroverts began to reveal themselves, I began creating the branches. I took students from each side and mixed them together. I mixed a few rule breakers with a few rule keepers, a few introverts with a few extroverts. This challenges the students to work with people different from themselves. It also keeps some degree of order. If I put all the rule breakers in one group, the process can become too chaotic.

We created four branches: blue, green, red, and brown. Now I can come in and say which branch we are climbing today and the students know where to go. Each branch has a healthy mix of personalities and learning styles.

We continued this process and made leaves which are triads. The triads are created from sub-groups of each branch. As in the initial branches, pay attention to putting diverse people together.

CHECK-IN AND CHECK-OUT IDEAS

A vital part of a healthy community and indeed a healthy life is pausing to "check in" and "check out." A conventional way to do this is with feelings cards or feelings posters. When students come in on Mondays and leave on Fridays, they are orienting from one environment (home) with one set of rules to another environment (school) with perhaps quite different rules. Checking in before these critical transitions can save a lot of time later.

When students don't have opportunities to verbalize, they often will "act out" things that are going on. This happens for kids from all types of homes. The most functional families have stressors. Even during the best school week you have ever had, things can happen that kids need to process. These simple tools also give kids the message that they have a voice. Giving them opportunities to express these things is in everybody's best interests.

Try these ideas and then generate your own.

- Check in with Far Side® cartoons—a hit at the middle school. "Which cartoon best fits your day?"
- Use the Body Parts Bag® from training-wheels.com. "Which body part best represents your weekend?"
- I have a bag of plastic insects from the dollar store that I use a lot. "Which insect best represents your weekend?"
- Use pictures of weather systems. "Which picture represents your mood so far this morning?"
- Gather a bunch of intriguing pictures from magazines. "Which picture represents your morning so far?"
- Make a number line along the length of your classroom. One is "bummed out." Ten is "fantastic." Have students distribute themselves along this line.
- Battery meter. Make an imaginary battery meter either on a poster or along the floor. "What's your energy level?"

You don't always need to get bad news. Good news is encouraged too. Whatever helps you connect with your students and your students connect with each other is a positive. At the end of the week, have them sit in a circle and share two pluses and one minus about the week. Make a visible record by putting their responses on a poster or chalkboard. This will help you and your students.

CHANGINGMESSAGE

None of us is as strong as all of us.

COOPERATIVE ACTIVITIES

FROM INSPIRATION TO ACTIVATION

The people I work with sometimes want to know where I get all my activities. Some I learned by experience, and then later I found them in books. Others I learned by reading about them. The activities I remember best are the ones I learned as a participant or created myself.

Kids often come up with variations. Doug Thiel and Brady Huffman were the inspiration for Gym Slalom. They were pulling each other down the carpeted hallway on laminated sheets of paper. We borrowed some pvc parts from Mr. Becker's still uncompleted irrigation project, and we had a slalom course.

Other activities (more than most other drivers might want to know about) are thought of during my drives to work. I do not have the average commute. Approximately 7 miles of my route is down a narrow and steep canyon without center lines or guardrails. I see eagles, deer, and four or five vehicles in a 45-minute commute. It's a good place to think.

With that in mind, here is an example of an activity from conception to creation to activation. I was sitting on a couch at the Lazy F Ranch where the Northwest Challenge Course Network Conference was being held. I was taking a break from the ice breakers and giving myself some introspection time. A woman who was only slightly less assertive than the highly assertive crowd of facilitators who had gathered there to share ideas said she had a game called "Zoom." Nobody seemed interested, or maybe they didn't hear her.

A man who had just led a diversity activity sat down on the couch and picked up the pictures that comprised the Zoom game. The pictures had been cut out of a children's book, and there were no words. The task was for a group of people to arrange the pictures in order without talking.

"These are cool," he said as he thumbed through them. "These are really cool!"

"Let me see!" I said.

He handed me some of the stack. They were cool! "I'm really excited about these! I am really excited about these!"

We never did play the activity at that conference, but my mind started working on it. I went through the childrens' books at home. They did not work because all the pictures had text on them.

Fast Forward. The kids in Michael Becker's class were restless. He was getting cranky, and they were getting resentful. They had just returned from Thanksgiving break, and the long, chaotic tube run to Christmas break had commenced. As I watched one student in particular, it occurred to me that, for certain learning styles, a desk is just a different kind of cage. As part of my commitment to creating and sustaining supportive learning environments, I put my brain into solution gear for the drive home.

After some dialogue, I convinced Michael to allow some of his more kinesthetic students to play with some non-intrusive manipulatives while they listened to speakers. I brought some Play-Doh®, a desktop sand tray, some Silly Putty® and, most popular of all, an exercise ball for one of them to sit on. I also threw in comic strip collections and a copy of *Road Kill of Middle Earth* by John Carnell. In order for them to keep the manipulatives, we stipulated that the toys must not distract the rest of the class, and the students must demonstrate retention of what was being discussed.

FLASH! The Zoom game idea would be perfect for this activity. After shedding some tears with the librarian, I cut some pictures out and laminated them individually. The words were on the back of each picture. I was concerned about the words being tempting to the audiences who might use them. Another FLASH! I remembered that the principal, in a brief-lived attempt to get me more organized, had given me a notebook containing the school schedules in transparent dividers. I had gratefully accepted the notebook, but somehow it ended up underneath the bags of ropes and fleeceballs in my office. Like a dog who always knows where the bone is buried, even months later, I found the notebook and placed the freshly laminated pictures inside the transparent dividers. I placed dark paper on the text side to block the words. I had created an activity that I could use repeatedly.

 STORYLINE

NEEDS: Pictures cut from a children's book with the text on the back of the pictures.

PROCEDURE: Distribute an equal number of pictures to each person. Tell them their task is to put the pictures in the order they think they should go. This can take a while. Shorter books (10 pictures) take less time. Students move the pictures around with the approval of fellow participants. Once they think they have them in order, have them read the text on the back to see if it makes sense. One way to do it is to have each student read the text from a picture.

FACILITATOR NOTE: Students will often insist that it makes a better story for the pictures to be arranged their way. I explain that we all have our own pictures in our mind. Some pictures we choose to ignore, some we choose to highlight. Everybody has a slightly different picture of the same event.

VARIATIONS: You can make this into an ongoing class initiative by placing the pictures along the whiteboard or a shelf.

OBSERVATIONS/QUESTIONS:
1. What are some of your favorite pictures or images from growing up (school, this summer, Thanksgiving, etc.)?
2. Are there pictures that you wish you didn't have? (Some laughs might result here.)
3. Show us a picture of you in ten years.

GYM SLALOM

Many Christmases ago, I had a German shepherd named Jasper. He was addicted to Frisbees® and tennis balls. In fact you couldn't say "Frisbee" without him going nuts and charging the door. Addiction ran in the family for sure. My dad and I were amusing ourselves by throwing a tennis ball across the linoleum kitchen floor and watching Jasper slide across the floor. The only people not amused were my mother and grandmother, who were cooking. Jasper was having a great time.

During the course of the cooking frenzy, garbage bags full of yucky stuff began to accumulate. I think I had been directed to take them out to the garbage can. I don't recall. After quite a few times of howling with laughter every time Jasper slid across the floor and pretending to be remorseful when Mom yelled at dad and me, the inevitable happened. Jasper bodyslammed the garbage bags. The fun ended with me picking up the garbage and trying to encourage the cat to climb the Christmas tree. That story has nothing to do with this activity other than that I often tell it before introducing Gym Slalom. It encourages kids to tell funny stories from their homes. Even the most dysfunctional families have many moments of joy and laughter.

NEEDS: You will need a rope that is at least 50 feet long and some slick 1' x 1' carpet squares.

PROCEDURE: Have your first volunteer stand with each foot on a carpet square and hold the rope firmly "tow rope-style" with both hands. Have everybody else hold on to the other end of the rope. When the skier says "go," everybody pulls hand over hand as quickly as possible. (For added fun, blindfold the skier.) After they safely get this down, tie in a rope that goes perpendicular to your pull rope. Have people on both ends guide your skier through a course of rubber chickens.

FACILITATOR NOTE: You can process this one if you want. Use your own best judgement. Sometimes when you're building community in the classroom, it's important to remember that fun is a basic need. The quickest way to turn kids off to Adventure Learning is to have long, drawn-out discussions after every activity.

Remind the participants to keep safety in mind. This game allows players to choose their own level of involvement.

OBSERVATIONS/QUESTIONS:
1. What guidance are you getting from your friends?
2. What guidance are you giving your friends?
3. What guidance do you think you need?
4. What guidance are you getting from the adults in this school, in your life?
5. What guidance do you want from the adults in this school, in your life?

BACK TO BACK

On a recent road trip a friend gave me a group development manual from 1969. Sure enough, activities similar to Back to Back were in there.

NEEDS: Both partners need a sand tray (an old lunchbox and sand from a recent trip to the beach), three marbles, and four toothpicks.

PROCEDURE: Have partners stand back to back. One of the partners makes a pattern with his sand tray and objects. He then has a specified amount of time to give a verbal description of his sand tray to his partner. The task is for his partner to recreate his configuration. There are quite a few variations of this. Try using pickup sticks, ropes (they cannot use known knot names), pine cones, rocks, or any arrangement of physical objects.

OBSERVATIONS/QUESTIONS:
1. What information did you receive?
2. How close was your arrangement to your partner's arrangement?
3. What directions were helpful?
4. What messages do you get about drugs and alcohol from your parents?...your friends?...the media?...your school?
(See how I slipped that in? Watch those coconut shells.)

ISLAND TAG

This game is not initially popular with some groups, but the thinking shifts it can create are valuable. After watching her class struggle with this game, a teacher said, "No wonder my kids can't pass the Student Learning Assessments; they have no critical thinking skills." I knew I had a convert. Few people learn critical thinking skills with pen and paper.

NEEDS: You will need enough webbing to lay out a 30- to 40-foot diameter circle, several Hula Hoops® (islands), and some throwables.

PROCEDURE: Lay out a circle that is 30 to 40 feet in diameter and place a Hula Hoop® (or other defined space) inside the circle. The person who is "it" has five throwables and must stay inside the Hula Hoop®. All other participants must keep moving inside the larger circle and cannot stay in one place for longer than five seconds. If the person who is "it" hits someone with a throwable, that person must join forces with "it" and stand inside a different Hula Hoop® that is added inside the circle at that point. I also appoint two retrievers to return the balls to the throwers until there are five throwers. When the throwers lose all their throwables, the game starts over with a new person in the Hula Hoop®.

FACILITATOR NOTE: This is a great game for teaching the value of planning. Depending on the size of the class, I will make the area bigger or smaller and adjust the number of throwables. Remember, head shots are illegal and ganging up is forbidden.

TRIANGLE TAG

PROCEDURE: Start with groups of four. Have the group members line up and join hands (three of the four will be holding hands). One person in each group is "it," and one person is the designated taggee. The task is for "it" to try to tag the taggee. "It" cannot jump across other group members as this is simply not safe. Allow each person in the group to try on the different roles. It's usually pretty difficult to tag somebody in this game. If your group looks like they're getting bored, have each group join with another group. Continue this process until it's one big circle and one person is trying to tag the taggee.

OBSERVATIONS/QUESTIONS:
1. What can we do to look out for each other or protect each other?
2. What can we do to help keep people safe?

A less mature group will often think of physical solutions. I try to get them to think about less obvious harms such as gossip and putdowns.

REFRAME OPTIONS
Let's say you are lucky enough to get some parents, teachers or community members in for a presentation. Begin the initial game, and assign a few common developmental assets to each triangle. As you bring them together and the assets multiply, they will quickly understand. (Refer to pages 69 and 72 to learn more about the Assets.)
1. What Developmental Assets do our children have in this community?
2. What Developmental Assets are we lacking in this community?
3. What Developmental Assets can we easily improve on?
4. One thing I am willing to do to increase an Asset is....

ALASKAN BASEBALL

NEEDS: A foam bat (noodle) and something soft to hit such as a kooshball, fleeceball, or other throwable.

PROCEDURE: In Alaska they love baseball, but it snows so much that a lot of times the bases get covered up. To make things simpler, they only use one base (home plate). Because they live in such isolated communities, they also have the rule that nobody strikes out. That way everybody always wants to play. To score a run, the batter has to run around his entire team. Each time the batter/runner makes one complete circumference around her entire team, that's one point. To get a person out, the team in the field has to pass the ball through the legs of each team member. If they drop it, they start over. When the last person gets the ball, he shouts out. Everybody gets to bat, and to ensure that people of all ages want to play, any contact with the bat is a hit. There are no "out of bounds." Since they are often low on money and supplies for months at a time, they use what's available.

After explaining all that, begin play. (I generally use a fleeceball and a foam bat.) There might be some initial confusion because the game only remotely resembles baseball. After two or three innings, or maybe just one, or whenever things are working up to a fevered pitch, I shout "STOP" when the game is at a tie. "In Alaska, because communities are so isolated and they want to make sure everybody continues to play, all games are played to a tie."

FACILITATOR NOTE: I generally don't debrief this. I just move on to the next activity and leave them pondering.

JENGA® CIRCLE

NEEDS: You can get Jenga® Blocks at just about any thrift store. Dollar stores carry a generic version.

PROCEDURE: Hand out three or four Jenga® blocks to each person and have them stand on them. Their feet cannot touch the ground. After it looks like everybody is uncomfortably but safely off the ground, I ask them what is the fewest number of blocks they can stand on. Often I will ask if I can take two or three more than what they've said. This gets them used to going beyond perceived limits. Afterwards, if necessary I will remind them that they went beyond what they thought they could do. Depending on the circumstances, I will often ask them to form a complete circle on the floor using only the Jenga® blocks. Then they must walk in a circle on top of the blocks. To achieve this they have to place hands on shoulders or in some way support each other. (See Jenga® Block Crossing on page 46.)

BUCKET LIFT

NEEDS: One 5-gallon plastic bucket per group of eight to ten participants, toothpicks, and pencils that you don't mind breaking.

PROCEDURE: Place a 5-gallon plastic bucket on the ground. Give each participant a toothpick. Ask one participant to lift the bucket using only a toothpick. Then ask two participants to try and so on until they are able to lift the bucket. The number of people needed will depend on the strength of your toothpicks. This is a simple activity to demonstrate that we often need the help of others to solve even simple problems.

Give a pencil to the strongest kid in class and have him break it. "Pretty easy huh?" Have him do two or three together. Then give him one pencil for each kid in the class and see if he can break the bundle. The man most Iroquois know as the Peacemaker used this example with arrows to demonstrate the power of a confederacy and the value of living in peace. Today that symbol lives on in the seal of the United States.

OBSERVATIONS/QUESTIONS:
What can we accomplish together that would be difficult to accomplish by ourselves?

BARREL OF MONKEYS

NEEDS: One Barrel of Monkeys® per group of eight to ten participants, and about 6 feet of string per person.

PROCEDURE: Place the smaller half of the barrel that contains the monkeys inside a Hula Hoop® or similarly sized webbing circle. Put all the monkeys but one in that half of the barrel. Tie strings about 3-4 feet long to one monkey. Have enough strings for every person. Some distance away, place the larger half of the barrel inside another Hula Hoop® or webbing circle. The task is for the group to move the monkeys from one half of the barrel to the other without dropping them. If they drop them, they have to start over. If that is too difficult, I have the class see how many they can move without recovering the dropped monkeys.

I've done this activity with kids as young as 2nd grade with great success. I usually limit the group size to six to eight participants.

FACILITATOR NOTE: As part of the facilitation process, I often have one member of the group drop his/her string and continue this until finally the monkey falls. Then I ask the question, "What happens when everybody does their part?"

I will also use fantasy with activities. "A group of monkeys is trapped on an island. You must rescue them. They are extremely frightened because they know a hurricane is coming. You must rescue them without touching them." Use your imagination to create your own story or metaphor.

RIVER CROSSING

NEEDS: 1' x 1' carpet squares or pieces of plywood.

PROCEDURE: The task is to cross an open space without letting your feet touch the river of poisonous, acidic peanut butter. You can only stand on these carpet squares. If one person touches the river, everyone has to go back. You can pick up your carpet squares, but it's illegal to just slide the squares along the floor. (They will get stuck in the peanut butter if you do that.) As usual we don't leave anybody behind.

The distance can be the length of a classroom or an entire gym. It depends on your group. I usually give out two or three fewer carpet squares than there are participants.

JENGA® BLOCK CROSSING

NEEDS: Jenga® blocks.

PROCEDURE: This is a paradigm shifter! I tell the class that I wanted to do River Crossing again but unfortunately I threw my squares in the dryer last night. They will have to use Jenga® blocks instead. Can they still do it? An alternative is to place the blocks in a circle. Have everybody stand on the fewest blocks necessary to get the entire group off the ground. After that is done, have them walk in a complete circle without anybody touching the ground. Usually they will have to physically support each other to succeed.

OBSERVATIONS/QUESTIONS:
1. Did this seem impossible at first?
2. Have you ever thought something was impossible but did it anyway?
3. Do we sometimes put unnecessary barriers on ourselves?

HULA HOOP® CROSSING

NEEDS: Hula-Hoops®. You can use old innertubes or rope/webbing circles.

PROCEDURE: This is another variation of the River Crossing activity. Again the group has to cross from point A to point B using only the Hula-Hoops®. Don't make it so short that the activity is not a challenge or so long that the goal is unrealistic. Another option is to have the group decide the length.

You can have as many people in a Hula Hoop® as will fit safely, but you can only have two feet on the ground at any given time. (This leads to some interesting solutions.) If any person touches the ground, the entire group has to return. The focus of this activity is how the group plans and how efficient the students are.

FACILITATOR NOTE: Inevitably your group will try piggybacking, linking hands in a chain or another cooperative venture. I have also had less advanced groups split the hula hoops up and have multiple solo adventures. In one middle school group, a student took all of the hoops and went over by himself. He then tried to throw the hoops back to his bewildered classmates. As if by the intervention of some divine hand, all the hoops landed out of the reach of his classmates. I couldn't have planned it better myself. Since this is often a beginning activity, the questions tend to focus on planning, goal setting, and inclusion.

OBSERVATIONS/QUESTIONS:
1. Was there a clearly articulated plan?
2. Who developed the plan?
3. Did everybody know the plan?
4. Did anybody have a plan they did not voice?
5. Were all ideas given equal attention?
6. What is "over there"? What are our goals? Why are we doing this stuff?

GROUP JUGGLE

NEEDS: At least five throwables.

PROCEDURE: Have the group stand in a circle. Toss a throwable to somebody across the circle. That person then throws it to a different person and the process continues until everybody has received the item and finally it comes back to you. Make sure everybody remembers who they threw to. Repeat the sequence if necessary. Add one item at a time until you have multiple objects in motion. The task is for the group to see how many items they can keep in motion. This is a good time to assess your group. If they try to shame someone for dropping the ball or messing up the sequence, you need to stay with the cooperative activities. This can be prevented with a little frontloading.

WARP SPEED AND TIME WARP

NEEDS: Two throwables and a stopwatch.

PROCEDURE: Follow the directions to Group Juggle, but stick with just one throwable. The task is for the group to throw the ball in sequence as quickly as possible. Any solutions the group comes up with inside of that parameter is acceptable. Records of 1 to 5 seconds are possible!

Try this paradigm shifter called Time Warp. Throw one ball in the original sequence. Throw another ball in exactly the opposite sequence at the same time. In other words, the person you threw one ball to is also the person you receive the other ball from. The task is to throw both balls in their respective sequences as fast as possible.

MID-AIR COLLISION

When you facilitate long enough, activities begin emerging from activities. During a game of Group Juggle using five rubber chickens, the chickens collided in mid air. A new activity was born.

NEEDS: One throwable for each participant.

PROCEDURE: Have the group stand in a circle. Give each member a throwable. On the count of three, have everyone toss their throwable. The goal is for their throwables to collide at some nebulous center spot and drop to the ground at the same time. I'd love to say more, but you just have to try this one for yourself.

TRIANGLES

NEEDS: Enough spot markers to make a pyramid. Pyramid numbers are 10, 15, 21, etc.

PROCEDURE: You have probably seen one of those wooden puzzles with golf tees in the shape of a pyramid. When one tee jumps a tee adjacent to it, the jumped tee is removed until you are left with only one tee. Try the same problem with human beings and it becomes infinitely more interesting. Using spot markers or sticky-pads, lay a pyramid out on the floor. Have the group stand one person per spot leaving one spot open. They can only jump in a straight line. The task is to get down to one human.

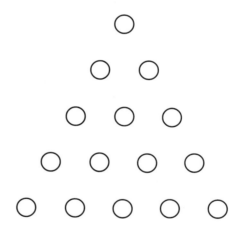

TRAFFIC JAM

NEEDS: One spot marker for each participant.

PROCEDURE: The people on the black spots must trade places with the people on the white spots. Mr. Smiley is an open space. There is one person per spot and they must stay in line! The only legal move is to move around a member of the opposite team. It is illegal to move backwards. Every time the group has to start over, the people at the front of their respective lines (the people closest to the happy face) go to the end, and everybody else steps forward. This allows the leadership to rotate and perspectives to shift.

FACILITATOR NOTE: If the group struggles a lot with this problem, I give them this hint. "Once you have started moving, if you are standing directly behind a member of your own team, you are stuck and have to start over." I also tell them to look carefully at each move before they make it.

OBSERVATIONS/QUESTIONS: This lends itself to great debriefing questions afterward. This activity is also a great frontload to a discussion about linear communication.

If you have a large group, split it into two groups. Once the group has mastered the moves, create a Crossroads Traffic Jam.

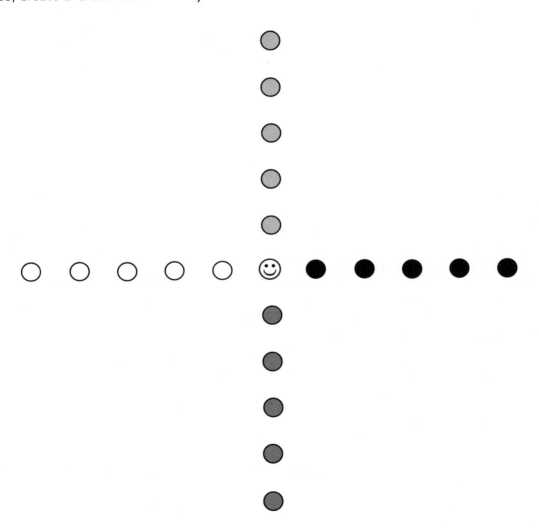

CHANGING MESSAGE

Trust is an egg. If we break it, we can put it back together again but only with considerable effort. It's much easier to design a system that will keep it intact indefinitely. What? No, Cody, we can't just hardboil our egg.

TRUST ACTIVITIES

Begin trust activities only when you are sure the group members are ready.

Are they skilled at cooperation?
Are there putdowns?
Do the group members treat each other equally?
Are conflicts handled openly and with respect for all concerned?

These and many more questions need to be asked and answered before beginning the trust sequence. Each group you work with will have its own processing pace and questions to answer. I frontload heavily with the group and remind them of the fragile nature of trust. We talk about the different kinds of trust and how trust takes risk. I usually end the discussion by stating that it will be difficult if not impossible to go any further unless we work on trust. What follows is a sequence that seems to work for me.

BLINDFOLD RUBBER CHICKEN TAG

NEEDS: One rubber chicken, boundary markers, and enough blindfolds for each participant.

PROCEDURE: This is essentially a tag game with a few notable differences.
- Set up clear physical boundaries.
- Divide the group into pairs. One partner is blindfolded. The other is sighted. The sighted partners give verbal directions but cannot touch their partners unless there is a safety concern.
- Ask for a volunteer to be "it." He should be blindfolded and hold the chicken. His task is to tag another blindfolded person who then becomes "it."
- Anyone who steps out of the boundaries at any time becomes "it."

- For obvious safety reasons, fast walking only—no running.
- After a reasonable period of time (a couple of minutes), switch partners.

OBSERVATIONS/QUESTIONS:
1. Which directions were helpful?
2. Can fun be a part of trust? Is trust a serious thing?
3. Did we stay safe during this activity?

 MIRRORING

PROCEDURE: Pair off in a creative way. Have partners face each other. One partner begins making any sort of movements and gestures. The other partner mimics every move. This usually generates some laughs. After a few minutes, switch. The purpose of this activity is to pay complete attention to another person. It is an invaluable skill for spotting and safety awareness.

 SPOTTING AND FALLING

The **spotting stance** looks a lot like what we used to call the pivot position. Feet are shoulder width apart. One foot is forward and the other is back. If these directions don't make sense, just ask a cheerleader or the cheerleading coach. See Teaching Tools and Resources.

The **falling stance** is sometimes harder to teach. A person's natural tendency when falling is to bend the knees and swing out the arms. Proper falling stance is to have arms crossed over the chest, feet close together, and legs stiff.

Go over these directions several times and don't allow anybody to fall until you have checked both stances. The spotter should stand directly behind the faller with his hands about 6 inches behind the shoulder blades. His toe should be right next to the faller's heel. At this point, ask the faller to say a phrase that will become very familiar over the course of the year:

> My name is _____.
> I take this risk willingly. Will you support me?

The faller needs to hear a resounding "Yes!" before he falls. Have partners practice this while you move among them checking and double checking for safety.

 WILLOW IN THE WIND

FACILITATOR NOTE: This activity is perhaps overused but worth repeating because it's effective if people haven't done it. Everybody should be well versed in the spotting and falling positions.

PROCEDURE: One person stands in the center of a circle of people who are all standing in the spotting position. (If you get any more than 10 people in the support circle, it tends be too crowded.) Have the person in the center ask for support.

My name is _____.
I take this risk willingly. Will you support me?

The faller needs to hear a resounding "Yes!" before she falls. She then falls at will in any direction. Ask that the group always keeps at least four hands on the faller. It's important to emphasize that people only do this if they choose. Do not allow anyone to be pressured into it.

 ## YURT CIRCLE

NEEDS: Retired climbing rope or 1-inch tubular, nylon webbing (approximately 3 feet of rope per participant). You can squeeze 20 people onto a 50-foot rope with the ends tied together. Tie the ends together in either a water knot for the webbing or a double barrel knot for the rope (see Teaching Tools and Resources). If retired climbing rope is unavailable, use rope with a rating to hold all the people. (Facilitator math: 15 people x 200 pounds each = 3,000 lbs.)

PROCEDURE: Have an even number of participants stand in a circle facing the center with both hands on the rope. Their feet should be shoulder width apart. When everybody's feet are firmly planted on the ground, have the entire group lean back at the same time. It's important that they use just body weight and not muscle strength. After the group has mastered leaning back without anybody falling, have them lean back and squat. It's CRUCIAL that everything be done simultaneously.

VARIATIONS: After the students have mastered the rope yurt circle, ask them if they're ready to go to the next step. If they are, have them drop the rope and count off by ones and twos. Have everybody grasp hands firmly but safely. Ones lean back while twos lean forward. Cool huh? Again synchronicity is vital. Then...reverse. Twos lean back and ones lean forward.

Mrs. Woods' 2nd grade class, after a few tries, had successfully completed the Yurt Circle with a rope. They had a little more difficulty with the "ropeless" Yurt Circle. Trying to keep things simple, I asked the class, "How were the two activities similar and how were they different?"

"Human beings are more fragile than ropes," replied Nicole.

"Yes, they are, so we need to be careful with them, don't we? Are we careful with the humans in our class?"

OBSERVATIONS/QUESTIONS:

1. What happens when just one person is out of step with everybody else?
2. What happens when we are all moving in the same direction?
3. Can we be moving in different directions and still working together?
4. Name some other times when we need to trust each other.
5. Tell me about the person you trust most in your life.
6. Have you ever lost trust in someone? What happened?
7. What makes you a trustworthy person? Is there anything you can do to become more trustworthy?

 RIVER

The intention of this activity is to create the feeling of gently floating down a river.

PROCEDURE: Form two lines and have the students face each other. They should be close enough so that a person could lie down on their outstretched arms. All the participants should be in the spotting position (one foot forward and one foot back). Arms of the supporters should be interlaced in a "zipper" fashion so as to provide complete support. When everybody's ready, have a volunteer lie down across the supporters' arms. When everybody is focused and quiet, pass the person in a gentle rocking motion to the end of the line. This can also be done kneeling. With a little frontloading, this can be an excellent closure activity.

 HUMAN LADDER

If we want students to shift their patterns, we have to be willing to shift our patterns.

NEEDS: One 3-foot dowel, 1 1/2 inches in diameter, per pair. At least nine people are needed to make this work.

PROCEDURE: Have the group form two parallel lines facing each other. Each pair should hold their dowel firmly between them, using both hands, so as to form a horizontal human ladder. Make sure that people hold the dowel so that it is resting in their palms. Demonstrate how easy it is to break a finger grasp. If they need to, they can rest it on their hips. They should be standing in the spotting position (one foot forward and one foot back). The task is for a person to crawl or walk across the ladder and arrive safely at the other side.

FACILITATOR NOTE: This is one of those activities that can cause injury if not done correctly or when a group is ready for it. When I begin with a class, I inform students that I may ask them to remove themselves temporarily from an activity. I ask them to step back, refocus, and recommit. This might happen when they use a putdown during a trust activity or violate the safety parameters.

I was facilitating Cindy Palmer's middle school PE class, and we were doing the Human Ladder. One boy and his partner were horse playing, and I asked them to step out. The first boy was familiar with my techniques and stepped back to watch. The second boy became angry (a pattern for him) and stomped off saying he'd rather just sit in the office. The principal and the discipline guy happened to be in the gymnasium at the time. They insisted that I needed to write him up (a pattern for them) so that he would respect my authority. I declined, which they respected. I had no "emotional currency" with that boy, and what I was asking him to do was beyond his range of experience. The next day we were doing the human ladder again. He joined us. I made no comment about the day before, and neither did he.

OBSERVATIONS/QUESTIONS:
1. How did we support each other during this activity?
2. How can we support each other all day long?
3. How do we make others feel supported?
4. How do we erode feelings of support?
5. Name one simple behavior you can change to increase the feeling of support.

 LIFTS

FACILITATOR NOTE: Have a volunteer lie down on the ground. Now tell him/her what's going to happen! Talk about choices and gathering information before you make any decisions. I have a strange gift(?) for getting people really excited and willing to do just about anything. By the time we get to this stage, kids are volunteering for everything. I use this teachable moment and review refusal skills. "You have the right to refuse anything that doesn't feel physically and emotionally safe."

PROCEDURE: Back to the volunteer lying on the ground. Now ask for at least seven more volunteers. (For an average person, have three people on each side and one at the head.) The person at the head should gently support the head and neck of the liftee. Have the three participants on each side form parallel lines and face each other. They should be close enough so that a person can lie down on their outstretched arms. Arms of the supporters should be interlaced in a "zipper" fashion so as to provide complete support. Review proper lifting procedure (legs not backs). Emphasize the importance of doing every move at the same time. This is one of those activities that can cause injury if not done correctly or when a group is ready for it. When everybody is focused and quiet, have the volunteer lying on the ground repeat the request for support.

My name is _____.
I take this risk willingly. Will you support me?

The liftee needs to hear a resounding "Yes!" before lifting begins. The person at the head does the counting. Make sure that the counter pauses and asks the lifters' and the liftee's permission to continue at 1) knee level, 2) waist level, 3) shoulder level, and finally 4) up over everybody's head. This accomplishes two goals. It allows people to participate at their own level of trust, and it allows lifters to make sure they have a good grip.

HUMAN 360

PROCEDURE: This is an activity you can do only after participants have a great deal of experience. It takes an advanced crowd to try this high-level task. After you have done quite a few lifts successfully, challenge the class to rotate a human being 360 degrees (head over heels) in the air.

Note of Caution: Human 360 should only be attempted by highly experienced and focused facilitators and groups. The facilitator should experience this activity through direct training with an accredited instructor before using it with a group.

WEB DESIGN

As a life principle, I must be willing to do anything that I ask others to do.

NEEDS: Approximately 400 feet of tubular webbing for a group of 15 people. I have a lot of webbing of various lengths, and I use most of it for Web Design.

PROCEDURE: Have the students form a circle. The task is to create a web that will support the weight of the largest person in your group. Usually that's me, and usually I am the first jumper. The setup can be a little tedious, but it's necessary for the metaphors to emerge.

Begin distributing the webbing around the circle and create a base. While passing out the webbing, make sure that each student is holding a loop and not just an end. Be sure to wrap the webbing around the existing strands with a clove hitch or similar knot (see Teaching Tools and Resources). This minimizes sag in the net.

The web is ready when there are no holes that a person can fall through. The participants should be leaning out in the spotting position and firmly gripping the webbing. It's a good idea to test the web first by tossing on a heavy object. The very first time I did this, we threw a 6-inch in diameter fence post on it. The confidence level of the students went up immediately. Have the participant stand beside the net and then leap from the ground up onto the webbing. After several people have jumped, have the group turn in a circle.

What happens as the process continues is that the web will begin to change. A once safe spot may not be safe anymore. Each jumper must examine the web closely before jumping. The web has shifting levels of support.

FACILITATOR NOTE: It would be easy enough to make a permanent web or to purchase one, but I like the issues raised by making one with the group.

Note of Caution: Web Design should only be attempted by highly experienced and focused facilitators and groups. The facilitator should experience this activity through direct training with an accredited instructor before using it with a group.

OBSERVATIONS/QUESTIONS:
1. What happened to the web as we continued to use it?
2. Did the support shift quite a bit?
3. Have you found this to be the case in real life?
4. Have you ever discovered support in areas where you did not know it existed?
5. Have you shifted your support in any area recently?
6. Have you ever lost support that you were really counting on?

If you are lucky enough to get a parent group or be invited to do a teacher in-service training, assign each part of the web a meaning.
1. How are we supporting the children in our community?
2. How are we supporting each other?
3. Are there holes in our support system?
4. What are the strongest parts of our support?
5. What can our support systems learn from each other?

VARIATIONS: When I was working directly in treatment as a chemical dependency counselor, I used the metaphor of the web a lot. I supplied paper, something to write with, and had my clients draw a "Recovery Web." On the different strands, they filled in the following:
Recovery Groups AA/NA
Clean and Sober friends
Counseling
Healthy Diet
Exercise
Positive Outlet (bowling, skiing, etc.)
Supportive Friends
Spiritual or Religious Practice

 TABLE TOP WEB

Several years ago, I was doing a presentation at the Washington Counseling Association Conference. They were trying to recruit chemical dependency professionals into their fold, so I was eager to make a good impression. In the brochure, I put Jeff Albin, NIBHN. Before I began my presentation, I asked them if anybody knew what those initials stood for. Most of them shook their heads "no." One rather serious fellow with quite a few initials behind his own name said, "I was thinking 'National Institute of Behavioral Health Network?'" "Well, no," I said. "It means 'No Initials Behind His Name.'"

Anyway, my presentation was on how to make portable low ropes activities for next to nothing. The prerequisites were "Advanced Scrounging" and "Psychobabble for the Intrepid Grant Writer." One of the items I brought was a scale model of a breakdown spider-web. It was about 18 inches tall and 3 feet long, made from 1/2-inch PVC and kite string. After the conference, I threw it in my bag of stuff and forgot about it. A few months later, I threw it in my car on a whim and brought it to work. Then, while I was blanking out at a staff meeting (almost as good as driving or the shower for idea generation), I came up with the idea of using action figures and/or a Barrel of Monkeys® with it.

NEEDS: To make your own portable PVC web of any size you will need the following PVC pieces. Don't be intimidated by the language. Any hardware salesperson should be able to assist you.
- Four "tees"
- Two 90-degree "elbows"
- Four "couplers"
- Lightweight string or elastic cord

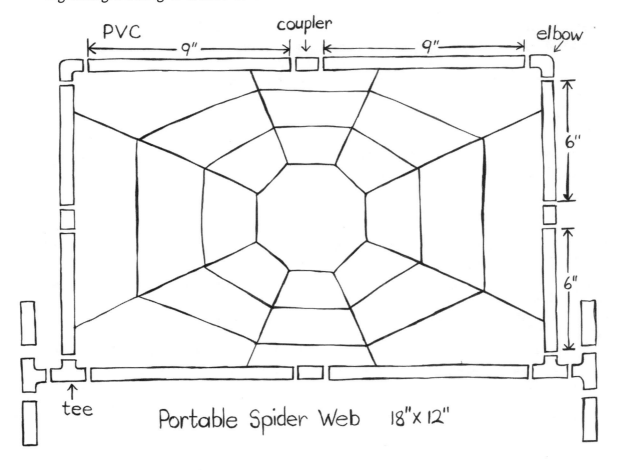

Portable Spider Web   18"x 12"

PROCEDURE: Here are the guidelines. Have one or two participants sit on each side of the web. The goal is to pass as many monkeys as possible through the web without dropping them or touching the web. Monkeys cannot be touched with the hands (they're radioactive). This doesn't necessarily need to be structured or debriefed. It's a casual toy you can keep in your classroom for transition times.

TWO-DIMENSIONAL WEB

The vertical web is more than likely familiar to most readers of this manual. Experienced facilitators tend to dismiss it because it is overused, but it still works for my students. It fits a sequence of learning how to do lifts and planning. I have seen quite a few horizontal webs, but I have not yet seen a double or two-dimensional web. To create a web, first engage your imagination. Then watch the movie "Entrapment" with Catherine Zeta Jones and Sean Connery. There's a scene with a very inspiring web. I have a portable version that is made from PVC and small bungee cord. I prefer to make my webs on the spot and have students assist me. It gives them a sense of pride and ownership in the activity.

Several years ago, I was asked to prepare some ATOD awareness activities for a school in Glenwood, Washington. I trained the Natural Helpers® to lead and debrief activities. We broke into small groups of 8 to 10 that were facilitated by two Natural Helpers®. The culminating activity was billed as the "World's Largest Spider Web." We created an enormous web across the width of the multipurpose room. We borrowed line from everywhere, including straps from ski racks. When it was all done, over 80 people had been through the web.

PROCEDURE: I make sure there are enough spaces so that there is one hole for each person. Find two trees that are about 12 feet apart and begin tying. It should be no more than a foot higher than the tallest person. After the first web is done, create another one about one foot away from the first. This presents an intriguing challenge. Spiderwebs and other activities that involve lifting can raise a lot of body issues. People who feel they are overweight or have been physically abused can feel quite intimidated by anything that involves touching.

FACILITATOR NOTE: Challenge by Choice (first articulated and copyrighted by Project Adventure®) in the wrong hands can quickly become "Challenge by Shame." I heard a reframe of the same concept from Erik Marter three years ago when we contracted with him to build a high ropes course in our gym. The term he uses is "choose your trust." Michael Becker uses the term "levels of involvement." In one school I work in, there is a young man who rarely participates in any of the activities I do. He does, however, watch intently and assists other students in attaining insights during the processing activities.

Whatever term I use, I make sure students get the message that they don't have to do anything that feels physically or emotionally unsafe. This effectively integrates refusal skills into my program.

OBSERVATIONS/QUESTIONS:
It's not uncommon during this activity for people to fail to plan effectively for the last person. This is where I often begin to process.
1. As you began your plan, did you think it through all the way?
2. Do you think it's possible that there are other areas of your life where you can't see the results of your decision?
3. Was being small or large an advantage in this activity? (Hopefully they can see the positives in each—small people fit through small, high holes, large people are necessary for lifting).

In addition to being a trust activity, the spiderweb can also be framed as an efficiency exercise. In your average middle school classroom, interruptions, body noises, and horseplay can waste a lot of time. The traditional approach is to simply squash the nonsense with office referrals, detentions, and suspensions. While effective in the short term, these measures tend to build alienation in the "Barts" of the world. Michael Becker uses my program as a tool for curriculum acceleration. He allots me a certain amount of planned time, and if the class stays focused and on task, they get "Jeff Stuff" in the afternoon.

1. Where was the group process efficient?
2. How can we cut back on wasted time?
3. If we reduced the amount of time we waste, what could we do with that time?

VARIATIONS: Somebody somewhere is still making those cardboard brick-colored blocks. I remember them from my childhood. Several years ago 4-H used a small mountain of them in some community building activities. If you are lucky enough to have them, you can make a block version of the spiderweb for elementary children. Keep it low enough so that they don't have to do lifts. The goal is to get everybody through without knocking the wall over. If you don't have blocks, I bet you have a lot of cardboard and maybe even a teaching assistant. Go find your teaching assistant and give her a straight edge, a ruler, and a lot of multicolored duct tape, and have her make a lot of blocks of various sizes. You and the students will find many uses for them.

PARTNER LEAN

PROCEDURE: Partners should stand, palm to palm, about 2 feet apart. Make sure they don't lock fingers. Have them step as far back as possible. Now try it in triads. Dyads?

WILD WOOSEY

When I first ventured into doing portable ropes activities as an avenue to prevention, I wrote a grant and purchased a kit that was supposedly portable. As long as you had a flatbed, it was most definitely portable. It included a bag with four 7-foot 2 x 6s and a smaller bag with blocks to support the whole apparatus. You can make several "elements" with it, and the quality is superb. Maybe it's age (I'm only 42) or maybe it's my restless spirit that gets tired of doing the same activities repeatedly (even if my audience hasn't yet seen them), but I got tired of toting all that stuff around. To make the lumber model yourself, refer to "Friendship Walk" in Chris Cavert's book *Affordable Portables*.

NEEDS: About 60 feet of tubular webbing. You could, however, just use masking tape on your classroom floor.

PROCEDURE: For a super lightweight Wild Woosey try this: Take that long piece of webbing and make a "V" that's about 12 feet long. Have the participants work in pairs to see how far they can progress down the legs of the V, starting where the legs of the V connect. They must stay in contact with each other at all times while staying on their own leg of the V. The challenge is to see how far partners can walk without falling. Don't forget spotters!

The Wild Woosey is an activity that will probably never go out of style. It's rich with metaphors, analogies, and symbolism. The only way to get to the end is to have partners lean completely on each other. The impact of that simple point cannot be overstated.

OBSERVATIONS/QUESTIONS:
1. What was necessary to complete this activity?
2. Does that have any application in this classroom?
3. Does that have any applications in life?
4. Who are the people you lean on when you need help?
5. Who leans on you?
6. How do you become a person that people can lean on or look up to?

 ### LIFE'S JOURNEY

Refusal skills and resiliency should be integrated into the curriculum and the Learning Agreement. Over the course of a year's programming, every child should have a chance to practice not doing an activity because it presents too much of a physical or emotional risk. It's important to honor children when they do this. Often, several students will want to do everything. Ask them to practice stepping out just so they learn the skill. "Minefield" aka Life's Journey gives everybody a chance to practice refusal skills.

NEEDS: I use just about the entire contents of my bag-o-tricks for this. On one impromptu occasion during a wilderness trip, we used pinecones for obstacles. I define the space with about 150 feet of rope in a circle.

PROCEDURE: Inside the defined area, dump your whole bag of stuff and create a maze. The difficulty level should match the ability level of your class. For a high-functioning class, put things close together and include the mousetraps.

After everything is spread out, have the class split into pairs. One person in each pair is blindfolded. The blindfolded person stays inside the boundaries. The sighted person is on the outside and can give only verbal directions. If the blindfolded person steps on anything, call "freeze frame," and ask him/her a question or pose a situation:

• An adult confronts you about something s/he thinks you did, but you know you didn't do it. You've had trouble with this person before. What do you do?
• Your best friend offers you a joint. What do you do?
• Your sister asks you to cover for her so she can steal alcohol from your parent's liquor cabinet. What do you do?
• Your buddies begin bullying another student. What do you do?

FACILITATOR NOTE: Be sure that the situations are realistic and match your audience. Unrealistic situations will only provoke cynicism. To get realistic situations, ask your students to generate a list of pressures and situations they face.

VARIATIONS: Ask for a brave volunteer. This person will be blindfolded and go through the maze alone. Only one or two people will be giving accurate directions. The rest of the class will be doing their best to give a lot of misinformation. The volunteer will not know ahead of time who is giving correct or incorrect guidance. This can create a lot of stress. Make sure the person knows that s/he can quit at any time.

OBSERVATIONS/QUESTIONS:
1. How did you know which voice to listen to?
2. In real life you get a lot of information. How do you discern who's giving out accurate information?

EGG DROP

I've been to more than one retreat where the facilitators began with trust activities and said, "Okay, now that we have established trust...." I am very careful and perhaps too slow to do trust activities, and I often don't frame them as trust exercises.

I had been working with one particularly turbulent class when I came up with the following idea. I often talked about trust as an egg. Keeping consistent with my principles of kinesthetic conundrums, I brought a real egg and wrote "trust" on it. I passed it around the circle while we talked about trust. "Trust is important. We need to trust each other if we want to grow. We need to become trustworthy people." I repeated a lot of the statements we often hear and say. Without any warning, I threw the egg up in the air and it fell onto the linoleum. It caught the teacher and counselor by surprise more than the students.

"What do we do now?" I asked.

"You need to clean up your mess," said several students.

"Does that seem like a good rule when somebody breaks the trust?" I asked. "How can we clean up the mess when trust is broken in the classroom? What if somebody keeps making messes? What do we do then? Do we allow people the space and time to clean up their messes? Do we make the mess bigger than it really is sometimes?"

USING ROLE-PLAY CARDS

Trying on a new role or seeing someone else in a role that you usually play allows one to make changes. Something about seeing somebody else in your role assists in the insight process.

Several years ago, I asked everyone in a class of 7th graders to try on a different role. The teacher and her most restless student agreed to switch roles. He became the responsible person and tried to keep everybody on track. She became the clown. We were just ending a session involving the human ladder. The "teacher," who had been acting responsibly all class period, was just getting ready to walk on the sticks. Suddenly, the "clown" started clowning around. The activity quickly fell apart, and class time ran out before the "teacher" had his chance. The next day we had a great discussion about humor and when to use it. That day sticks in memory as an example of the power of role playing in an experiential setting. I don't recommend role plays early on in the process, but use your own best judgement.

Within this section are three different kinds of role-play cards. One set is Oppressive Behavior Cards. Another set is Inclusion Behavior Cards. You will find Family Role Cards on page 94. I encourage you to use them in a creative fashion.

FACILITATOR NOTES: I've seen and used role-play/role-change activities in more ways than I can remember. In the past, I did it just during a single class period. More and more, I am asking students and staff to try on a new behavior all day long. I would not recommend this with the Oppressive Behavior cards. The negative roles are good only in the short term followed by an effective debriefing. Allowing students to focus on a single positive behavior all day long will help them integrate change at a pace they can handle.

OBSERVATIONS/QUESTIONS:
1. What was it like to try on a new role?
2. Did playing a different role help you understand anybody better?
3. Do we allow people to change behaviors, or do we prefer to keep them in their roles?
4. What healthy behavior would you like to take on more often?
5. How can the class assist you with that goal?

TALKING when necessary & LISTENING when necessary.	PAYING ATTENTION to PROCESS instead of always worrying about ACHIEVEMENT.
WAITING until people have SPOKEN before giving INPUT.	LISTENING to others' input & BUILDING ON IDEAS.
SPEAKING in assertive tones to express ideas & ACKNOWLEDGING OTHERS' opinions.	LISTENING carefully to feedback & working toward positive CHANGE.
Looking to SEE how IDEAS might WORK.	Being RESPONSIVE to the NEEDS of individual members.

Phrasing FEEDBACK in a way that others will HEAR.	LOOKING for the POSITIVE in all SITUATIONS.
Letting others TRY OUT LEADERSHIP roles.	LISTENING completely to each speaker before RESPONDING.
Seeing the value in VIEWPOINTS DIFFERENT from one's own.	STAYING present, alert, & aware even when uncomfortable subjects such as FEELINGS are broached.
RESPECTING opposite genders & DIFFERENT cultures.	Seeing PEOPLE as PEOPLE, not as objects.

Sharing LEADERSHIP willingly.	SHARING information, resources, & IDEAS freely.
Speaking only for oneself, MAKING NO ASSUMPTIONS about others' thoughts.	INCLUDING all people when-ever possible REGARDLESS of race, class, gender, status, religion, etc.

OPPRESSION CARDS

GRANDSTANDING: Talking too much, too long, & too loud.	PROBLEM SOLVING: Continually contributing before others have a chance.
Speaking in CAPITAL LETTERS: Using aggressive tones to declare that one's opinions are the final word on the subject.	DEFENSIVENESS: Responding to every contrary opinion as if it were a personal attack.
NIT-PICKING: Pointing out minor flaws in statements of others.	STEALING THUNDER: Restating someone else's idea, particularly a woman's, to the group as your idea.
ATTENTION SEEKING: Using dramatics to get the spotlight.	TASK & CONTENT FASCIST: Insisting on adherence to a task or to process at the expense of nurturing the group.

PUTDOWNS & ONE-UP-MANSHIP: "I used to believe that, but now..." or "How can you possibly say that?"	**NEGATIVISM:** Finding something problematic in everything.
BACK-SEAT DRIVING: Hanging on to former positions of responsibility.	**SELF-LISTENING:** Formulating a response after hearing a few sentences, not listening to anything from that point on, & leaping in at the first pause.
GEORGE CUSTERISM: Taking a stand for one's position on minor items.	**DENIAL:** Intellectualizing, withdrawing into passivity, or making jokes when it is time to share personal feelings.
CONDESCENSION & PATERNALISM: "Now do any women have anything to add?"	**BEING "ON THE MAKE":** Using sexuality to manipulate.

RUNNING THE SHOW: Continually taking charge of tasks before others have a chance to volunteer.	**POWER BROKERING:** Protectively storing key information for one's own use & benefit.
SPEAKING FOR OTHERS: "A lot of us think that we should..." or "What so and so really meant was..."	**EXCLUDING:** Removing people from activities because of race, class, gender, religion, or other social grouping.

Leadership doesn't mean doing it all your-self or focusing only on the goal. Leader-ship means helping people get where they want to go.

INITIATIVE ACTIVITIES

David Hawkins, Ph.D. and Richard Catalano, Ph.D., researchers from the University of Washington, came out with a list of Risk and Protective Factors around substance prevention several years ago (www.drugabuse.gov/NIDA_Notes/NNVol16N6/Risk.html). It's pretty dry and does not apply to all communities. Later, researchers with Search Institute developed a list of 40 Developmental Assets (www.search-institute.org/assets). The thinking around both models is easy to understand. The Risk and Protective Factor model demonstrates that the more protective factors a community has, the fewer problems the children will experience. The Asset model demonstrates that the more assets children have, the less likely they are to experience severe problems. The Frog Wars and Bell Ringers activities are easily framed to help kids understand these concepts.

FROG WARS

NEEDS: Enough lily pads (carpet squares) for each person to have one. (To increase the challenge, give them one or two fewer lily pads than the number of people. This can raise interesting scarcity issues.) As many throwables as you can muster. Rope or webbing to use as boundary markers for the road.

PROCEDURE: The fantasy scenario for this game goes something like this: "A family of frogs is happily living in a pond. Life has been good. There's plenty to eat, everybody's happy, and there are few if any problems. One morning the frog family awakes to find that construction has begun on a super highway that goes directly through their pond. This highway splits the frog family in half. The task is to reunite the frog family safely. The only safe way to cross the highway is by using their magic lily pads.

Some cars have already begun using the freeway, but right now traffic is pretty light. Once a frog gets across and knows the way, it no longer needs the magic lily pads. In fact, it can go freely about the highway and even stop cars. It knows the way through the danger spots.

Divide the group into cars and frogs. Each group will have a chance at both roles. The frogs try to get across the freeway using only their magic lily pads. The cars try to stop the frogs from getting home by throwing things at them. If a frog steps off his lily pad or gets hit by a throwable, he must begin again.

Frog rules:
  • If a frog is stepping from one pad to the next and gets hit, the frog has to go back.
  • Frogs with both feet on one pad are safe.
  • The lily pads are movable.
  • Only one frog per pad.
  • When a frog has gone all the way across, it is "magic." It can block shots!
  • No frogs are left behind.

Car rules:
  • Cars cannot walk on the road to retrieve their throwables, but they can use any item on their person to retrieve them.
  • No head shots or ganging up on one frog.

FACILITATOR NOTES: I usually give each group a certain amount of planning time, and then the madness begins. It's not uncommon to have the cars lose all of their throwables in a brief flurry. Another typical result is that the frogs will begin to stockpile the throwables out of the reach of the cars. A "magic" frog will often do this. As the group is happily progressing toward safety, watch how they do what they do. It's not uncommon for one person to take two pads and charge forward independent of the group (the "hero" model).

I am careful with the "start over" approach. With a highly functioning group or even a group that still doesn't understand the "co" in cooperation, everybody starts over. With other groups, just one person goes back. Sometimes, I will send back a person other than the one that was hit to emphasize the group aspect of the task. With a flexible group, I might move the "safe" zone 10 feet or so back just as they almost reach their goal. This can lead to discussions about how goals can often change or become more difficult than they originally appeared.

OBSERVATIONS/QUESTIONS: This chaotic exercise is rich with metaphors and analogies. Typical questions I might ask are:
  1. What can we do to protect each other from all the negative things that are out there?
  2. What resources do we have to help keep each other healthy?
  3. What sudden unexpected change (the highway) has occurred in your life?
  4. Did you need help when that happened? How did you get/seek help?
  5. Did anybody offer help when you needed it?
  6. Who would you go to in your school or community if you really needed help?

VARIATIONS: When working with a group of middle schoolers, I often use a different scenario. I ask them what pressures teens face. For every response, I throw a sheep or fleeceball into the center of the circle. The answers you might expect may include: drugs, parents, homework, dating. The participants don't know what's going on, but they know that every time they come up with a response another throwable appears. After the bag of sheep and fleeceballs is distributed, I explain the rules.

BELL RINGERS

I learned this game from the fine folks at Team Synergo. It's similar to Frog Wars, but the outcome is often different. As of this writing, I haven't frontloaded it with any particular information. I just give the kids some very basic rules and let them go. When the activity is over, I backload with questions that seem to fit the experience.

NEEDS: Each team gets a bell that is tied to a string. (I prefer bear bells, available at most outdoor stores here in the Northwest. For quite a while I borrowed bells from the music department. A good friend of mine who operates a thrift store gave me a big bag of Christmas bells, and now I'm busy inventing new games with bells.) As many soft throwables as you can gather.

PROCEDURE: Divide your group into two teams. Have each team choose one member to tie the bell around his/her waist. (If you prefer, have them tie the bell to something that is held. That way the person isn't being targeted, but what they are holding.) Divide the soft throwables between the teams and instruct them to try to ring the other team's bell using the throwables. Send the teams to opposite ends of the area of play. A basketball court is ideal. Then have each team try to get to a circle in the center first without ringing their bell.

FACILITATOR NOTE: Due to the nature of this activity and the fact that I highly encourage alternative thinking strategies, a group may try to step outside of the rules too far. I will pause the group and tell them that while I really appreciate the "out of the box" strategy they have devised, I want them to stick with the rules.

The "Rules" are the constant values of a supportive learning environment. They include respect, commitment, healthy communication and the other elements of our learning agreement. Any deviations from the rules of an activity must be mutually agreed upon by all participants. This can happen quite spontaneously. It's important as facilitators that we adapt quickly to rules that make sense and fit the situation.

I have seen quite a few strategies in this game even though I have only been using it for about six months. It's not uncommon for teams to launch a full out barrage of throwables at the other team while giving scant protection to their person with the bell. It's "the best defense is a good offense" strategy. One long-legged boy just spread his legs far apart and ran without the bell ringing. A small, quiet girl took advantage of the ensuing chaos and ran to the center before anybody even noticed her. Both were "strength strategies."

OBSERVATIONS/QUESTIONS: The questions following this activity might be similar to Frog Wars.
1. What kind of strategy was used to protect the bell holder?
2. How was the bell holder chosen?
3. What were you doing to protect each other from negative things?

 CONNECTIONS

I was sitting in a day-long training on the topic of tobacco, and my mind began to wander. The trainers were essentially offering two strategies: education and cessation. I began thinking about all of the systems that need to be intact and functioning in order to raise a healthy child. How do we get to the point where a child starting to smoke is universally viewed as unthinkable? While this is by no means an exhaustive list, it's enough to get the point across during this activity. It fits in well with Assets and Risk and Protective Factors.

1. Family
2. School
3. Community
4. Faith Communities
5. Media

6. Peers
7. Extracurricular Activities (sports, band...)
8. Food Systems, Nutrition
9. Health Care

It can be a little slow-moving for middle school groups. I have found the greatest success with this activity when I use it with parents, teachers, or community groups when I'm trying to explain my model. Using the above list, label each system (group). Each system that interacts with another is then linked. Hopefully family is linked to school. When all the systems are linked in a way that the participants feel best fits their community, have each group tie the ends of their rope together.

NEEDS: Each group gets a 15- to 20-foot piece of tubular webbing or rope. The length of your webbing or rope will vary with the size of your group.

PROCEDURE: Tie the ends of one length of webbing (system) together to make a circle. Take the next piece of webbing, bring one end through the first circle, and tie the ends together so that you have two circles linked together. Continue this process until you have created a chain of connected circles.

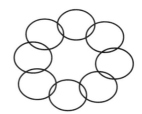

For a much more difficult process, create a Venn diagram with your webbing circles. Begin with the first two circles interconnecting. The difference will be that each circle connects to all the other circles related to the group.

When it's all set up, you will have several groups holding onto their individual circles. Each participant has a "death grip" (for lack of a better term) on his/her circle. While holding onto its webbing circle, each group in turn must rotate through all of the other circles to which it is connected.

Some groups will want to slide the knot without moving their bodies. Their bodies must move with their webbing circle. When each group has made one complete circle, the activity is done. You can time it if you wish, but the complexity of this task usually leads to discussions about the connections we have with other people.

- Each loop must make one complete revolution.
- Participants' hands cannot move once the activity begins.
- Each complete revolution represents one day.
- The goal is to get through one day. (If we try to live too many days at once, it becomes overwhelming.)

FACILITATOR NOTE: Inevitably, whether you are dealing with kids or adults, somebody will not understand the directions. That person (or persons) will try to just pass the rope in their hands without moving (surely there is a metaphor here). I insist that each person move with the ropes. People may also be linked to different systems. To illustrate the food/nutrition system, I have collected the containers from a typical child's lunch in their community and tied them to the food loop. This has included pop cans, doughnuts, potato chip bags, and candy wrappers. It makes a nice visual and can lead to a lively discussion.

OBSERVATIONS/QUESTIONS:
1. Which systems are linked or unlinked?
2. Which systems do we need to improve?
3. If we were going to work on just one system, which would we choose to work on?
4. Is that what we want to do?

VARIATIONS: This activity can be too complex for younger children. It can be done with just two loops to talk about conflict, or you can give each child a short rope and have them just move the knot as a way to show how they are all connected.

 DOMINOES

I just started using dominoes this year, and I am beginning to see some real potential. They provide a subtle tool for quick mixers, learning teams, and random partners.

In a traditional classroom, if I ask the children to pick a partner, inevitably they will gravitate toward their best friends. A general, unoffical hierarchy already exists. Some kids are popular. There might be one or two who are ostracized. Hopefully there are a few who transcend the invisible barriers. When I ask for random groupings, there may be some resistance. A middle school boy once informed me that he was worried about being with the people who weren't "cool" because he was afraid the "uncool" would rub off on him. When I see this type of resistance, I employ a few tools from my toolbox that seem to work most of the time. Usually what I will do is break out a fun game that everybody wants to play. I inform the partners that they are free to join or not to join, but if they chose to join they must do so with the partner they have.

DOMINO ACTIVITY #1

NEEDS: A set of dominoes. I have this groovy set of extra large foam dominoes I purchased from Training Wheels. They have a great visual appeal but they are definitely not kid proof. Most schools already have dominoes somewhere in the building. If all else fails, check your nearest thrift store.

PROCEDURE: Distribute the dominoes randomly. The task is for each person to find a partner by matching the ends of their dominoes. For example, if one person has a two and a five, she must find a person with either a two or a five. The only parameter is that within 3 to 5 minutes, each person must have a partner. The activity is not finished until everybody has a partner. If there is an uneven number of people, I join the activity.

FACILITATOR NOTE: What I have experienced multiple times is that pretty quickly, most people have a partner and one or two people are left drifting. Even if the partners are not best buddies, they are reluctant to separate. A static moment might follow when the group is "stuck." The critical leap occurs when enough people recognize that they must look beyond their own domino in order to help the group be successful.

 DOMINO ACTIVITY #2

NEEDS: A set of dominoes.

PROCEDURE: Depending on group size, the next task is to have four to six people connect. It is not uncommon for the class to experience the same phenomenon as when they tried to find a partner. More movement is required to achieve "success."

DOMINO ACTIVITY #3

My bureaucratic turkey button has just popped. —Michael Becker

NEEDS: A set of dominoes.

PROCEDURE: The task here is to make one continuous chain. That's all I tell them.

Recently, I was doing a presentation at the Washington State Prevention Conference. The conference is typically a pretty dull affair. I'm the token fun guy. Most rooms are filled with people doing PowerPoints on the seven principles of this or that. My first presentation was in a room adjacent to the supply room which fortunately or unfortunately was unlocked. There was a whiteboard with the words "Welcome, Washington Sheepherders" that I liberated and placed outside my room with one of my throwable sheep. I also found a genuine chalkboard which I quickly moved to my room. I used this for my "PowerPoint" presentation. With my imaginary clicker I showed my slides:

Slide 1: Here are some rather shocking statistics from our latest survey.

Shake your head, point your finger, and say "What are we going to do?"

Slide 2: Here are some hopeful statistics based upon our recent work.

Hopeful look and head nodding

Slide 3: Here are the Seven Principles of Mediocrity from the Office of Suspicious Public Inevitability. (The State of Washington's education department is called the Office of Superintendent of Public Instruction)

Slide 4: Here's a quote from Albert Einstein: "The significant problems we face today cannot be solved at the same level of thinking which created them."

Much laughter (spontaneous and unprompted)

Slide 5: Here's a picture of me receiving a phone call from my boss on Monday: "Jeff!!! What were you thinking making fun of OSPI in public?"

After my empowering PowerPoint presentation, I distributed my dominoes and asked the group to make one continuous chain. Several people simply gave theirs away.

I asked one woman, "Do you always give away your power like that?"

She went back to the person to whom she had given her domino and rejoined the activity. It was a powerful moment for both of them. The person who had received her domino, a young man in cowboy boots, jeans, belt—complete with an enormous rodeo trophy belt buckle, shirt with pearly, white buttons, and cowboy hat had a teachable moment. Although he was a teacher committed to experiential education, he related to the group that he often violated his own principle of letting the students learn on their own by helping them solve problems when they were "stuck." The woman told us that it was not uncommon for her to remove herself from group tasks at work just to avoid the hassle. They both committed to work toward changing these power-diminishing behaviors.

I have experienced this phenomenon with students also. The questions I typically use focus on this theme.

OBSERVATIONS/QUESTIONS:
1. What does it mean to give away your power? You can give away your power to anger, drugs, negativity.
2. What is "power"? If the group is focused and interested enough, I will explain William Glasser's notions on basic needs (love, belonging/acceptance, freedom, fun, power/competence)
3. What can you do to keep your "power"?
4. What is your "strength strategy" when you have a problem to solve?
5. What is your partner's "strength strategy"?
6. Would your partner's "strength strategy" work for you? What can you learn from that strategy? Are you willing to try it?

KING'S FINGER

NEEDS: You will need at least six 5-gallon plastic buckets with lids. Remove the metal handles. Use a small tire for the ring.

PROCEDURE: A popular and low-cost feature on low ropes courses is an element called King's Finger. It consists of an 8- to 12-foot vertical wooden pole. At the base is a car tire. The tasks are simple. The first task is to remove the tire without touching the pole. The second task is to put it back. If you are using this low-ropes version, add a couple of spotters for safety. However, I most often use a cheap, portable version of this activity that can be made from plastic buckets with lids on. Stack as many buckets as the group is uncomfortable with and ask them to remove the tire (ring) without touching (or knocking over) the buckets.

> "You are a band of little people who have crashed your plane in the land of the giants. The giants are a fearsome race and will eat you if you are discovered. One giant has the only key to their airplane attached to a ring on his finger. If you can successfully remove the ring without waking the giant, you can make your escape."

VARIATIONS: Get one of those inflatable pool rings and use that instead of a tire. One that has a whimsical attachment such as a duck's head can lead to another story. You can also use a piece of webbing or a Hula Hoop®. To add an additional challenge and pull in more students, attach several bells on strings to the ring. Blindfolding several participants can also add challenge. In keeping with the fantasy story, you could also "mute" your class.

 ## BELL WALKERS

Tyler Williams is an elder from the Dite Da Nation on Vancouver Island. He is also a spiritual teacher and a Sundancer. One of the things he does with people who come to him for guidance is ask them to tie bells on their shoes. They walk with these bells until they can walk effortlessly without making noise.

NEEDS: One foam bat, at least one blindfold, a generous amount of throwables, and a whole lot of bells.

PROCEDURE: Place a blindfolded person in the center of a rope circle that also contains a foam bat and a bunch of throwables. All the other players must have at least one bell tied to their shoes. The challenge is for the blindfolded person to defend their "treasure." Every time the blindfolded person touches a player with the foam bat, that player must return all of the items s/he has removed from the rope circle.

FACILITATOR NOTE: I generally don't debrief this activity. Sometimes we do stuff for fun. The class that plays together stays together. It can be an opportunity to see how your class is progressing on safety. This is an elaborate version of Marco Polo.

As I said earlier, I don't use foam bats with students younger than 11 or 12. With middle school students, the bats are a great way to teach boundaries. If somebody plays too roughly, they just don't play.

VARIATIONS: To add another twist, the person in the center can ask for a person without a blindfold to give verbal guidance.

GUIDANCE CHUTE/SHOOT

Like a lot of experiential educators and ropes course trainers, I have an eye for finding intriguing materials that I might be able to use in activities. A wonderful source of materials is your local military surplus store. At one store, I came across a small parachute that had a few built-in holes. I think it was a guidance chute for a larger chute. The built-in holes made most people look at it skeptically. One of Michael Becker's students asked if it was actually a parachute. Michael said, "Yes, but it was an experimental model that was only used once."

NEEDS: A 50-foot piece of tubular webbing or rope and a parachute. If you don't have access to a parachute, improvise with a tarp or sheet.

PROCEDURE: Have the group stand in a circle around the parachute (which is spread out on the ground). Have the group hold onto the rope that has been tied into a circle. Now ask them to get everybody underneath the chute without letting go of the rope. If that works without major collisions and your group is safety conscious, have each member put his/her head through a hole. This is a good activity to time for a common goal.

VARIATIONS: With a much larger rope circle, place enough paper grocery bags in the center of your circle so that there's one for each person. If you're feeling ambitious you can put a character education word on each bag or a group goal that everybody has agreed upon. Still feeling ambitious? Don't worry; it will pass. The task now is to get a paper bag on each person's head without letting go of the rope or using any part of their hands. It is a good ideas to have each person select the bag they are going for before they proceed.

FACILITATOR NOTE: Have one safety monitor for each six people. This is a good task for observant introverts who think all this stuff is nuts.

BULL'S EYE

In a popular activity called "Inside Out," the participants are asked to go underneath a rope on the ground without using their hands and arms. I've used this activity with everybody from kindergartners to teachers. One of the goals of my curriculum is to develop a strong set of critical thinking skills. While a given set of problems might look quite similar, in actuality they can be entirely different problems.

"It's been a long week, and I know that you are all itching to get back to your comfort zone." (The bull's eye resembles the "comfort zone" concept that they are already familiar with.) "Even getting back to your comfort zone, however, might require some uncomfortable manipulation. You may find a change in your comfort zone as a result of this activity. All you have to do is get everybody to the inner circle without touching the ropes with your arms or hands."

NEEDS: Three lengths of rope that are 1/2 inch or greater in diameter. The lengths of the ropes will vary with the size of the group. For a group of 10 to 15 people, the ropes will need to be long enough to make circles 8, 12, and 16 feet in diameter. I tie all of my ropes in double barrel knots so that I can quickly adjust the size of the circle to fit the activity.

PROCEDURE: Lay three concentric rope circles on the ground so that they look like a "bull's eye." The task is to get everybody to the inside circle without touching the rope with their hands or arms.

FACILITATOR NOTE: It's not uncommon for someone to want to put the rope in his mouth. For hygienic reasons this is not allowed.

VARIATIONS: While the comfort zone is often presented as a means of learning by venturing outward, I actually see it as just the opposite. Many times as we journey further inward, the difficulty magnifies. I will present this concept to the group and see which makes more sense to them. Have the group start in the inner circle and get to the outside. This activity can be presented with or without frontloading.

OBSERVATIONS/QUESTIONS:
1. Was the problem of the first circle the same as the problem of the second and third circles?
2. What strategies did you use?
3. What was similar about the situations you encountered with each rope? What was different?
4. Did the same strategy work in all three situations?
5. Have you ever used the same strategy for problems which were similar on the surface but different once you dove into them?

FOUR DIRECTIONS

I have a bag full of 6-foot pieces of 1-inch blue webbing that came with the "Adventures in Peacemaking" kit from Project Adventure®. They did not come with instructions, so I just invented some activities that utilize them. This activity is (hopefully) another paradigm shifter.

NEEDS: I use five 6- to 10-foot lengths of webbing tied in a circle because that's what I have. You can use string, carpet squares, or anything that defines a space. For Phase 2 you will need a long piece (100 feet) of 1-inch tubular webbing or retired climbing rope.

PROCEDURE: Place five small circles on the ground. The first circle is at the center. The other four circles are placed in four opposite directions and adjacent to the center circle.

Instruct participants to evenly distribute themselves in each circle. The task is for the participants in each circle to move to the circle immediately across from them. They must stay at least 3 feet above the ground until they arrive safely on the other side. Encourage them to focus on safety, efficiency, and planning. (The participants in the center circle, stay in the center circle.)

FACILITATOR NOTES: The solution that most groups arrive at is lifting students one by one into the opposite circles. The group in the center circle generally does the bulk of the lifting. I have seen more creative solutions, but as much as I would love to share them, I need to leave you with some surprises. The goal is seemingly straightforward, but by adding the requirement of efficiency, this seemingly simple problem leads to more discussions about problem solving.

PHASE 2

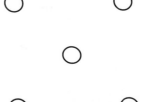

Move the hoops far enough apart so that the most agile participants cannot just leap into the circle. Give the group a retired climbing rope or a 100-foot section of 1-inch tubular webbing. This problem is best suited for advanced groups. (The problem is the same as in phase 1, the solution is different.)

FACILITATOR NOTE: It seems like the trainer's world often consists of dividing people into quadrants. Reframe the four exterior spots as Myers Briggs® types or the colors from the True Colors® personality test. The four colors are often framed by Lakota people as representing the four primary races of human beings. Sensing any possibilities?

VARIATIONS: In the Lakota world view, there is a concept about the cardinal directions known as the Cangleska (pronounced Changleshka). Different *tiospayes* and *tiwahes* (bands and families) have different understandings of this concept and what each direction means. Please don't interpret this as the final definition. It works for me.

> West / Black / This is the color of looking within.
> North / Red / This is the direction for seeking wisdom.
> East / Yellow / This is the place of growth.
> South / White / This is the place of death and birth.

I am careful not to impose my spiritual beliefs on the audiences I work with, but I believe there are some common threads with which few people would find difficulty. Looking within, wisdom, starting over, and death are universal ideas from which all people can benefit. A simple framing tool uses the four Ws.

Within—What do I see when I look inside?

Wisdom—Where have I found wisdom? Which people in life provide me guidance?

Wonder—What things do I marvel at? What unanswered questions do I have? What questions do people have about me? Is there mystery and awe in my life?

Without—What am I lacking? What do I need to let go of? What assets can I see in somebody else that they cannot see themselves?

 TP SHUFFLE

In more than one ropes manual you can find a description of the TP (telephone pole) shuffle. Participants stand on a fallen tree or a horizontal telephone pole and must rearrange themselves by birthday, shoe size, height, etc. without touching the ground. I include this activity here to show what you can do with equipment you already have. Most of the playgrounds out here in the great Pacific Northwest have borders made of treated 6 x 6s. Have your class stand on one, mark some boundaries, and have them shuffle. Depending on the difficulty of the situation, you may need to use spotters.

VARIATIONS: For younger children, place two ropes on the ground about 2 feet apart as the boundaries. Now have them switch places. Too easy? Keep moving the ropes in and have them repeat the activity.

 ORCHARD ENGINEERS

Credit Vince from the Cispus Challenge Course, who credited a group of engineers from Port Orchard, for this one.

PROCEDURE: Have the participants stand in a circle. They will create three patterns. The first pattern begins with one person saying another person's name. This continues until everybody's name has been said. Practice this name sequence until they are sure everybody has it down. The second pattern starts with one person looking across the circle at another person and naming his/her favorite food. Practice this sequence. For the third pattern, yet another person starts. This person walks across the circle, touches another person on the shoulder and takes that person's spot. That person moves one spot to the right, causing the next participant to move, etc. Continue until it gets back to the person who started it. The final task is to complete all three sequences as quickly as possible.

 ROPE TROLLEYS

Trolleys are these rather cumbersome ski-type affairs which the group is asked to walk with from point A to point B. For instructions on how to make a durable pair get Karl Rohnke's book *Cowstails and Cobras*. They're generally effective but have been overused and are really heavy. Following are a few alternatives along with some activities which teach the same concepts.

BICYCLE INNER TUBE TROLLEYS:

Partner up and have each pair lift the inner tube to about waist level without using their hands. Now have them walk in a mutually agreed upon direction toward a common goal while keeping the inner tube at waist level (still without using their hands). How was that decided? (To get inner tubes, go to your local bike shop in the spring and summer and ask for their discards from fixing flats. Beware the tubes with green goo on the inside. I cut out the valves before distributing the tubes.)

SHORT WEBBING TROLLEYS:

Tie short pieces of webbing into circles. This is pretty much the same as Inner Tube Trolleys, but the dynamics change because of the materials used.

LARGE GROUP WEBBING TROLLEYS:

Take 50 feet of rope or webbing and lay it on the ground with the ends tied. Have the group lift it to waist level without using their hands. Now walk toward a mutually agreed upon direction, keeping the rope or webbing at waist level.

CHAIN GANG:

Take a 40-foot piece of 1-inch multi-line (cotton clothes line would work) and have the group use their hands to place it on their shoulders. Have them walk toward a mutually agreed upon goal, keeping the rope on their shoulders without touching it.

HULA WALK:

Place a Hula Hoop® on the ground. Each participant can only touch the hoop with one finger. (Eight is probably the maximum for this activity.) Have them raise the hoop from the ground with each person using just one finger. Now have them turn in a circle. Feeling confident? Challenge the group to flip the hoop without dropping it.

STRAW CONNECTION:

Beg some straws from the cafeteria. (Get twigs from a willow tree. Chop up the tentpoles from that old tent you really need to retire. Grab a whole bunch of pencils from the Navy recruiter next time she shows up. Adapt, improvise, overcome.)

Have the group stand in a circle. Each member of the group holds a straw using only their index fingers so that the group is standing in a circle connected to the participants on either side of them by straws. Make the circle as big as possible without dropping the straws. Shrink the circle as small as possible. Make a figure eight. Now form the Bill of Rights (just kidding).

 FRAMING IDEAS

I first encountered the formalized notion of "mental models" in Peter Senge's book *The Fifth Discipline*. Previously, I had used similar notions as an English teacher when I was teaching "Point of View." During any of the Trolley activities try this:

1. Have your students close their eyes and visualize a tree.
2. After their eyes are open, put up pictures of four quite different trees: pine, maple, cottonwood, bonsai.
3. Now ask them to move toward the picture which most closely matches the tree they visualized in their head. It can get pretty interesting at this point, especially when the group moves from two people to 10 or more.

OBSERVATIONS/QUESTIONS:
1. What ideas do we share as a class?
2. What ideas do I share with my partner?
3. What ideas do I have that are different from my partner's or class'?
4. Are the differences we have a strength or a weakness?
5. How did you decide which direction to move?
6. Did anybody move in a direction that they really did not want to go just because it was less hassle? Have you ever done that in real life?

REFRAMING RUDOLPH

On the day before Thanksgiving break, I was joking with a teacher at Klickitat that, while I was looking forward to a fine feast the next day, I was a little worried about Christmas since we had barbecued Blitzen the year before. She told me not to eat Rudolph. How would the reindeer reach their goal without him? I started thinking about the elements of the Rudolph story.

Rudolph was an individual with unrecognized strengths. The organization came to depend on him to such a degree that it was convinced it could not perform without him.

Who are the Rudolphs in this class?

Fast forward. It's the 21st century. Rudolph has been recruited by a headhunter from the Kwanza Commandoes, a focus group that wants to make Kwanza as big as Christmas.

Rudolph is leaving for sure. What will you do for leadership now?
Is our class dependent on "Rudolph" or a few individuals to achieve group goals?

BANDANA BALANCE

NEEDS: One bandana for every two people and at least two small items to place in the center of the bandana.

PROCEDURE: Divide into pairs, and give each pair one bandana. Have the partners hold the bandanas by the corners. Place an object in the center of each bandana. Encourage them to move around the room and toss the object up and down without dropping it. After they seem to be proficient at that, have them switch objects with another pair using only the bandana. When the class seems to have bandana balancing skills down, bring everyone into a circle and have them practice moving multiple objects continuously around the circle without dropping them. I use soft objects for this. Some roll easily and consequently get dropped. Other items don't roll at all. Ask the class if they want to see how quickly they can get all the objects around the circle.

OBSERVATIONS/QUESTIONS:
1. How many things do we have going on in this classroom?
2. How are we balancing those things?
3. How many things do you have going on in your individual life?
4. How are you balancing those things?
5. What happens when we get out of balance?

 ## TOWER ACTIVITIES

I don't recall how many different tower activities I've seen and how many ways I've used them. The materials can vary with your audience. I have two large bags of cut-up foam noodles (dots) that are quite popular with elementary teachers and students. They're colorful, and when the tower falls, no harm is done. Remember the number-one rule when helping people is "First do no harm." The first rule of working with elementary teachers is not to create any more ruckus in the classroom than you have to.

PROCEDURE: In a typical elementary classroom, towers might be one of my first activities. I distribute a roughly equal number of whatever we are stacking to each small group. For example, in Rene Davis' combined 2nd and 3rd grade classroom at Klickitat Elementary, the desks were clustered in groups of four. I walked around with my bags of dots and made little piles on each cluster. In some groups, I put equal piles on each desk. In others, I placed them all at the intersection of the desks. Then I instructed them to build the tallest tower possible with only five points of contact. I deliberately left the instructions open-ended, as I usually do. What happened next was to some degree predictable. One student who has difficulty sharing hoarded her dots. Other students quickly caught on and tried to collaborate or asked if they could collaborate. A particularly troublesome student came up to Rene to complain that the other students were not listening to his ideas. A simple tower activity had quickly become a diagnostic tool. Plato was right again!

OBSERVATIONS/QUESTIONS:
1. Did anybody think about sharing to make a really big tower?
2. What would happen if we combined all of our dots?
3. Do we want to make sharing a classroom goal?

VARIATIONS: With an older group, have students sit in a circle in groups of four to six around a pile of tower building objects that have a lot of texture and variety. Tinkertoys® are a good choice for this. The goal is to build a tower as high as possible. Each participant, in turn, adds one piece. They cannot talk or in any way influence the choice of other participants. Give them a time limit. This can vary with the maturity level of the group. Afterwards, have them discuss why and how they made each choice.

Instead of asking the class to build the highest tower possible, ask them to create a structure (without talking) that represents them as a whole. This can lead to some interesting discussions afterward when you ask why and how each choice was made.

 MOUSETRAPS

This is definitely **not an activity for elementary-age youth**.

NEEDS: Enough mousetraps so that each person has one. I also carry several extras along with a bag of spare parts. Mousetraps are not very durable.

PROCEDURE: I start with a single mousetrap and go through a laboriously detailed explanation of how to arm and disarm a mousetrap safely. I point out that as long as my fingers are not in the danger zone, where the cheese would be, I will be okay. I tell them multiple times to grasp the mousetraps only underneath and in the safety zone. After I feel confident that everybody understands, I distribute the traps and urge them to practice setting them safely.

The first activity I do after I make sure that everybody has "mousetrap safety" down is actually a trust activity. I demonstrate that by putting my hand palm down directly on top of the trap and pulling it straight up without sliding it forward or back, I can disarm the trap without injury. Then I find a volunteer to guide my hand while I am blindfolded and I disarm the trap.

The second activity is to set as many traps as possible and pass them around the circle without setting them off. I follow all this with a discussion.

FACILITATOR NOTE: I ask the class to think about being in the danger zone and in the safety zone. Sometimes I talk about the "rush" they feel when they hear the traps snap. (This is a good activity to follow Genogram on page 100 at the end of the ATOD activities.) This activity may feel too risky for some participantsis. Allow players to choose their own level of involvement.

MOUSETRAP STACKING

NEEDS: Mousetraps.

PROCEDURE: Divide the group into pairs and have each pair make a mousetrap tower with as many mousetraps as possible. All of the mousetraps must be set. Erik Marter, who gave me this idea, says the world record is nine, which he and an accomplice achieved at the latest AEE Conference in Vancouver, British Columbia.

FACILITATOR NOTE: Towers present obvious metaphors. You can easily relate goals and dreams to the structure. On more than one occasion, I have had groups opt for creativity instead of height. Like the dominoes activity, groups in the early stages of development might splinter with a few individuals completing the activity and others standing idly by. A simple solution is to create smaller groups. Another strategy is to employ "hazards" or "penalties." This can include muting the more verbally dominant members, blindfolding one or more people, tying two members' hands together, or simply pulling aside the more boisterous members and giving them instruction on leadership: "Leadership doesn't mean doing it all yourself or focusing only on the goal. Leadership means helping people get to where they want to go."

Tower materials I've used so far include: balloons and masking tape, newspapers and scrap paper, dominoes, bottle caps, mousetraps, cardboard bricks, straws and old library cards, Legos®, Lincoln Logs®, and old computer pads.

 WATER SUPPLY

If I can't use it, it is most definitely junk. –Michael Becker

Before his irrigation system was in place in his class garden, Michael and his students had to carry water by 5-gallon buckets to the newly transplanted trees. I watched and participated in this process, and it was becoming drudgery. Surely moving water could be more fun. What if we could make it into a fun efficiency initiative?

NEEDS: Several 1 to 3 foot pieces of 2-inch diameter plastic pipe with caps on one end. I scrounged them from the local natural gas supplier (they hadn't been used). Drill a lot of finger-sized holes at random intervals in each section of pipe. Several 5-gallon buckets.

PROCEDURE: Break into small groups. The challenge is to move the water from one 5-gallon bucket to another as quickly as possible. Inevitably the students will try to see how much water they can move onto each other. It isn't necessary to process this one. When community (common unity) is being created, it becomes apparent.

FACILITATOR NOTE: It's hard for me to tell the difference between cooperative activities and initiative problems. Maybe there isn't any difference. I define an initiative problem as "a task that requires the entire group's cooperation to solve." For some groups, a cooperative activity may be quite challenging.

REMOTE DRAWING

NEEDS: A big, fat marker, plenty of string, scissors, duct tape and some basic line drawings. (In a novelty store, I found a fat pencil that's over a foot long and about 1 inch in diameter.)

PROCEDURE: Take a blank piece of paper and tape it to the ground inside a circle. Give one person a line drawing for the group to reproduce (this person is the only one allowed to see the drawing) and have that person stand next to the circle. The rest of the group should be far enough away that they cannot see the drawing. Now attach one 6-foot string per person to the marker using the duct tape. Tie a knot close to the end of the string and tell them they cannot touch the string beyond that knot. The person with the drawing must give directions to the "artists" so that they can recreate the original drawing.

VARIATIONS: Two people are given the paper with the drawing on it. (I often use a drawing of a circle, a triangle, and a square placed next to each other or perhaps even intersecting.) They describe the drawing to two other people. These two will then tell the people with the strings and marker what to draw. They cannot use terms that name the objects involved. For example, if the drawing is a circle, they cannot use the word "circle." They must only use concrete directions.

For a simpler task, have your group write somebody's name or just a letter.

FACILITATOR NOTE: Two themes often emerge from this activity. The first is what I call detailed communication. Detailed or specific communication is a skill that can take a lifetime to master. One of your student communicators might say "make a short line going that way." Challenge that person to change the direction into specifics. "You need a two inch straight line about 10 inches from the edge of the paper by John's foot."

The second theme is how difficult indirect communication can make things. Schools are often plagued by gossip. The first variation of this activity can dramatically illustrate how easy it is to keep the information straight.

 CONSENSUS

Consensus is perhaps one of the most valuable activities I teach. It's a good back door to bullying education.

NEEDS: I use Mr. Potato Head® and his accessory case. The accessory case has perhaps 50 different pieces. You can also use Tinkertoys®, Legos®, or anything with a lot of variety and appeal to different learning styles.

PROCEDURE: One person at a time has a chance to add one piece to the potato. Once a person puts a piece on, s/he explains their choice. Each person in the class has the opportunity to agree or disagree to the addition. If there is a single disagreement, it doesn't stay on. The person choosing the piece asks, "Well, can you live with it?"

If everyone agrees, it stays on. When a piece generates a lot of discussion but no agreement, it goes into the "hot pile" in the center. These are "tabled" issues. People will often want to move into a "voting" mind set. Explain the difference between consensus and democracy. The 4th grade class at Klickitat, a very process-oriented crowd, spent nearly 4 hours of their own free will on this activity.

 KNOTS

NEEDS: Rope

PROCEDURE: Tie a square knot in the center of your longest rope. Have everybody grip the rope with both hands. The task is to make the same knot without letting go of the rope. Done yet? Try a double barrel knot.

 FORCE FIELD

NEEDS: Rope.

PROCEDURE: "The aliens have trapped you in a force field. They are arriving in 15 minutes to take you back to the mother ship for scientific experiments. You can touch the force field, but not with your hands. Get out quick!"

The "force field" is a rope tied in a circle lying on the ground. The task is to get everybody out as quickly as possible. In order to get out, they must go under the rope without using their hands. Do it several times and challenge the group each time to improve their speed. After they have mastered this task, have them try to get back in.

 FIGURE EIGHT

NEEDS: One 50-foot rope.

PROCEDURE: Take your 50-foot rope, tie the ends together, and form a figure eight on the ground. Split your group in half in some creative fashion. Have the two groups step into the circles that have been formed by the figure eight, one group in one circle and the other group in the other. Now, without touching the ground on the outside of the circles, have them switch.

PARALLEL LINES

NEEDS: Two pieces of rope.

PROCEDURE: Lay two ropes parallel on the ground about 3 feet apart. Before you tell the group what the task is, have them step into the space between the ropes. Now have the group arrange themselves by birth date. That should be easy. Now move the lines so they are 2 feet apart. Keep decreasing the width until it becomes a real challenge. Allow the group to create their own challenge.

STAR OF DAVID

NEEDS: A 100-foot rope tied in a circle.

PROCEDURE: I preface this by saying that I have no hidden agenda by using a religious symbol. The activity was first presented to me using a five-pointed star. That has negative connotations for quite a few people. The Star of David seemed safer because it's usually well known.

Have everybody grasp the rope circle. The task is to create a Star of David. This can be a complex task.

 ROPE SHAPES

NEEDS: Rope.

PROCEDURE: Blindfold everybody. If they don't want to be blindfolded, they can participate but cannot speak. Ask people without blindfolds to be active observers. The task is to create a square using a rope. If that's easy, try a banana, an apple, or a double helix.

RUBBER CHICKEN LAUNCHER

In late spring after the bike repair shops have fixed a lot of flats, they always have a lot of inner tubes. I pick up a big bundle of them for this activity. Beware of the tubes with slimy green goo.

NEEDS: I give each group of four to six kids about eight tubes, 6 feet of webbing, one rubber chicken, and a tape measure. I always make sure to cut out the valves before I distribute the tubes.

PROCEDURE: The task is simple. Each group must make its own rubber chicken launcher. I usually bring my very official 100-foot contractor's tape to measure the results.

FACILITATOR NOTE: Although this is generally just a fun activity (something about seeing a rubber chicken airborne seems to lighten people up) it can be used in a variety of ways. A low-functioning team will have just a few people doing most of the work while others stand by and watch. With the levity created by the rubber chicken, I can ask the group members to rate their level of involvement on a scale of 1 to 10.

OBSERVATIONS/QUESTIONS:
Does your level of involvement reflect real life, or was it just this activity?

TARP TURN

NEEDS: I generally use an 8 x 10 or 5 x 7 tarp, but you could use an old Twister tarp or even a sheet. Using a sheet with cartoon characters can add some lightness to the situation.

PROCEDURE: Have a group of 8 to 10 people stand on a 5 x 7 tarp. The task is to turn the tarp over without anybody touching the ground. If they master that quickly, divide or fold the tarp in half and have them try it again.

VARIATIONS: To see if your class moves quickly to cooperate, have two groups within jumping distance on two different tarps.

FACILITATOR NOTE: There are some obvious metaphors in this activity about "turning it over." If your group is stuck in the "storming" stage you can frontload with a discussion about negativity. The "up" side can represent dissonance, conflict, and putdowns. The "down" side can represent cooperation, support, and constructive feedback.

RICOCHET BALL

In most PE catalogs you can find an item called a ricochet ball. These balls have several bumps and bounce in multiple directions. At our friend, the dollar store, you can often find similar balls. For a comprehensive guide to ricochet balls, get *Ricochet* by Chris Cavert (book and balls available at Fundoing.com).

NEEDS: Ricochet balls or any balls that bounce erratically will work.

PROCEDURE: The first activity is to throw the ball in the air and let it hit the ground. Each bounce equals one point. If the ball "flatlines," there is no point. The catcher asks for a low, medium, or high toss (approx. 10, 14, and 20 feet, respectively). The goal is to get as many points as possible. I usually do this in a circle, one pair at a time.

VARIATIONS: After the group has some idea of how to use ricochet balls, I divide them into groups of four or five and give each group a webbing loop about three feet in diameter. The task is similar. All group members have to hold the webbing loop except the thrower. The last bounce must go through the loop. This is a great teamwork activity.

FACILITATOR NOTE: On yet another of those magic days, I brought out my ricochet balls and started some activities. The teacher ran back into the classroom and returned with three different reaction balls he had recently purchased. Each had different bouncing characteristics. We made up several games on the spot. At the end we put all the different balls in the center and asked the kids to go around the circle and tell which ball their life was most like. The reaction to that simple question was powerful. Just like the balls, the lives of several of those kids were highly unpredictable.

OBSERVATIONS/QUESTIONS: I will often follow this activity with a brief discussion about risk.

1. What is a healthy risk?
2. What is an unhealthy risk?
3. What is a perceived risk?
4. What is a calculated risk?
5. Why is it important to take risks?
6. Why is it important to understand what kind of risk you are taking?

 ## STARCHY EDIBLE TUBER HEAD (SETH) ACTIVITY

This book might better be called "Teaching with Toys." One of my favorite group toys is Mr. Potato Head®. (I am unclear about trademark laws and regulations, although the makers would undoubtedly be excited about my promotion of their product.) From here on out, I will call him SETH.

NEEDS: One SETH product of both genders (Mr. and Mrs.) and enough blindfolds for 15 participants. If you have a large class, you can divide it up and double your props.

PROCEDURE: Have the group sit in a circle. On the SETH boxes, there are pictures of the characters with all their body parts in place. Pass these boxes with the pictures around the circle. I usually pass Mr. clockwise and Mrs. counterclockwise. Instruct the participants to memorize the picture on the front of the box. Give them adequate time to become familiar with the picture.

Pass out the blindfolds. Remind the group that no one has to wear a blindfold. Those not wearing blindfolds cannot speak. If a group member removes his or her blindfold at any time during the activity, that person can no longer speak and is asked to actively observe the process.

Once everyone has their blindfolds firmly in place, have them hold out their hands. Pass out the body pieces along with the two SETH bodies. Have the group assemble the SETHs exactly like the pictures they saw on the boxes.

Sit back and watch the fun. This is a great activity to videotape for later review.

FACILITATOR NOTE: This can be a highly charged activity. A group that has been struggling with communication or what I call "the illusion of communication" may hit the wall on this one.

Lessons come around repeatedly, until we learn them well. When we learn one lesson, along come people who are learning the same lesson. How we help them learn defines our character.

ATOD SPECIFIC ACTIVITIES

Back when I was a river guide, there was a rating system for rapids. I do not remember all the particulars, but it went something like this.

Class One—You can run this on an innertube.
Class Two—Tubing might be okay, but use your brain more.
Class Three—Way fun, big waves. Guiding skills necessary.
Class Four—Stop and scout. Danger ahead.
Class Five—Experts only. The price of poor planning could be disastrous, even deadly.
Class Six—Waterfalls. Unrunable except for people from the lunatic fringe.

When I venture into family stuff with any group of people, I approach it at least as a class-four rapid. I pull my raft onto the beach and scout carefully. I try to have three plans.

Plan A: The preferred course.

Plan B: Less desirable but still runable.

Plan C: I will need all of my skills to negotiate this course. I will be under extreme stress, as will my passengers.

THIS IS LIFE

FACILITATOR NOTE: I frontload this activity by asking the class for definitions of the word "conflict." After a brief discussion, I give a working definition while emphasizing that this is only my definition: "Conflict is two ideas trying to occupy the same space and time."

NEEDS: I usually use a kooshball and a hackysack.

PROCEDURE: Ask everyone to be seated on the floor in a circle, leaving a space for you. Phase One: The facilitator passes the hackysack to the participant on his/her left and says, "This is life." The person who receives the hackysack asks, "What?" And the facilitator repeats, "This is life." That person passes it on to the next person saying, "This is life." And so on. This sequence is repeated until the hackysack goes all the way around the circle. This may sound confusing, but just remember that "This is life" goes to the left and "What?" comes back to the facilitator.

Phase Two: Repeat the same sequence as in Phase One. Add the koosh ball by passing it to the right and saying, "This is addiction." The passee asks, "What?" Repeat, "This is addiction." The sequence continues.

Eventually the two objects will collide, and some chaos will ensue. I let this continue until it has passed the point of usefulness. Both objects should return to the facilitator, but this doesn't always happen.

OBSERVATIONS/QUESTIONS:
1. What happens when life collides with addiction?
2. Did anybody experience strong feelings? When have you experienced this feeling before? (It's not uncommon for people to become angry, controlling, storm out, etc.)

 ## ENDLESS CIRCLE

NEEDS: Approximately 4 feet of heavy string per person. In both ends tie loops large enough for a person's hands to fit into comfortably.

PROCEDURE: Put people into pairs. Partner #1 puts both loops on his/her own wrists. Partner #2 takes his/her string and puts one of the loops on one wrist. He then takes the other end, passes it around his partner's string, and puts the second loop on his other wrist. They are now connected. (Imagine two people wearing handcuffs in such a way that they are both connected.) The challenge is to get free without removing the loops from their wrists. YES, it's possible.

FACILITATOR NOTE: After they've struggled for a while, give the first hint: "Everything you are doing now is not working." Usually this is greeted with laughter or unfriendly looks. After some more struggling, announce, "You can do this sitting down" or "It's all in the wrists" or "There are four openings; just go through one of them."

Sometimes, after the group has struggled and nobody has solved the problem, I give one randomly selected pair the solution. I then tell them that they can do whatever they want with the information. How they handle this is talked about during the debriefing. If everybody has solved it but one pair, be sensitive to those potential issues. This may be a good time to talk about how it feels to be left out, etc.

VARIATIONS: After everybody has figured it out, have them all link up and try to get free (up to 15 participants). This is a good time to talk about enmeshment, boundaries, and the feeling of being trapped within a system.

OBSERVATIONS/QUESTIONS:
1. How is this similar to addiction?
2. Where does the problem lie?
3. Where does the solution lie?
4. The AA definition of insanity is "Doing the same thing over and over again expecting different results." How does that apply in this situation?
5. Was my first hint useful? Did people keep doing the same thing?

SIMPSONS' LECTURE

Fortunately or unfortunately, most young people are familiar with "The Simpsons." They provide a convenient and familiar model for the alcoholic family. Claudia Black, John Bradshaw, and other family systems pioneers discovered that alcoholic and other types of dysfunctional families shared certain consistent traits. One of these traits was that the children in these families tended to fall into "survival" roles. Each role provides a certain function for the family. (See Family Role Cards on page 94.) For more information visit the National Association for Children of Alcoholics Web site. For simplicity, the Simpsons fit neatly into the following roles:

Bart is the scapegoat/mascot.
Maggie is the lost child.
Lisa is the hero.
Marge is the codependent.
Homer is the alcoholic.

PROCEDURE: I have done this in a variety of ways. Sometimes I lead a brainstorming session and ask the class to describe "The Simpsons" characters one at a time. Other times I split the class into five groups and have each group come up with a list of characteristics. When the lists are done, no matter how you do them, describe the roles of the chemically dependent family. Credit Kara Seaman with this idea.

Each role provides a certain function for the family. It must be emphasized that these are "survival" roles.

Bart, as the scapegoat, provides a way for the rest of the family to distract from their own issues. If most of the energy is going toward fixing Bart's problems, there is little time for anything else.

The family can point to Lisa, who gets good grades and is almost a model child, as proof of their success and functionality.

FAMILY ROLE CARDS

SCAPEGOAT — bart

Visible Qualities: VISIBLE SUCCESS, DOES WHAT'S RIGHT

Inner Feelings: LONELY, CONFUSED, INADEQUATE, ANGRY

Family Functions: IDENTIFIED PROBLEM CHILD, IRRESPONSIBLE

Characteristics: HIGH ACHIEVER, SCHOOL JOCK, COMPANY MAN, SOCIAL NICE GUY, GOOD GRADES, FRIENDS, SPORTS

Future w/out Help: WORKAHOLIC, NEVER WRONG, RESPONSIBLE FOR EVERYTHING, MARRIES DEPENDENT PERSON

Future w/Help: GOOD PROBLEM SOLVER, RESPONSIBLE FOR SELF, GOOD EXECUTIVE

MASCOT — bart

Visible Qualities: HUMOROUS, FRAGILE, IMMATURE, NEEDS PROTECTION, HYPERACTIVE, CLOWN

Inner Feelings: FEARFUL, INSECURE, CONFUSED, LONELY

Family Functions: COMIC RELIEF

Characteristics: HYPERACTIVE, LEARNING DISABILITIES, SHORT ATTENTION SPAN

Future w/out Help: ULCERS, INABILITY TO HANDLE STRESS, COMPULSIVE, CLOWN, MARRIES "HERO" FOR CARE, REMAINS IMMATURE

Future w/Help: TAKES CARE OF SELF, NO LONGER CLOWN, FUN TO BE WITH

LOST CHILD — maggie

Visible Qualities: WITHDRAWN, LONER, ANGRY

Inner Feelings: WITHDRAWN, SULLEN, HURT, LONELY, GUILT, FEARFUL, REJECTION

Family Functions: RELIEF, DOESN'T CAUSE PROBLEMS

Characteristics: INVISIBLE, QUIET, NO FRIENDS, FOLLOWER, TROUBLEMAKER, DAY DREAMER

Future w/out Help: DEPRESSION, SEXUAL IDENTITY PROBLEMS, PROMISCUOUS OR ISOLATED, DIES YOUNG

Future w/Help: INDEPENDENT, TALENTED, CREATIVE, IMAGINATIVE, SELF-ACTUALIZED

HERO — lisa

Visible Qualities: DOES THE "RIGHT THING"

Inner Feelings: LONELY, CONFUSED, INADEQUATE, ANGRY

Family Functions: SUPER RESPONSIBLE

Characteristics: HIGH ACHIEVER, SCHOOL JOCK, GOOD GRADES, DEPENDABLE

Future w/out Help: WORKAHOLIC, NEVER WRONG, OVERLY RESPONSIBLE, MARRIES DEPENDENT PERSON

Future w/Help: CAN ACCEPT FAILURE, GOOD LEADER, RESPONSIBLE FOR SELF, NOT EVERYBODY ELSE

ALCOHOLIC — homer

Visible Qualities: ANGRY, DEFENSIVE, CHARMING

Inner Feelings: SHAME

Family Functions: IDENTIFIED "SICK ONE"

Characteristics: VARIES FROM "TOWN LOSER" TO "COUNTRY CLUB CHARMER"

Future w/out Help: UNTIMELY DEATH, DIVORCE, INCARCERATION

Future w/Help: HELPFUL, HIGHLY SPIRITUAL

CO DEPENDENT — marge

Visible Qualities: HAS IT ALL TOGETHER

Inner Feelings: FEARFUL, INADEQUATE

Family Functions: CONTROLING, PROTECTIVE

Characteristics: NEEDY, CLINGY, OBSESSIVE-COMPULSIVE

Future w/out Help: UNTIMELY DEATH, CANCER, ABUSE VICTIM

Future w/Help: POWERFUL PERSON, ROLE MODEL

Adapted from Claudia Black and Sharon Wegscheider Cruse with sincere apologies to Matt Groening.
Changing the Message © 2004, Wood'N' Barnes Publishing & Distribution, 800-678-0621

Maggie is the kind of kid that teachers love, mainly because she causes no outward disruption. She provides the same function for her family. She can disappear in a room full of people.

Marge is primarily addicted to Homer's alcoholism, and, as one of my students put it, "tries to hold the family together."

Homer, as the identified screwup and alcoholic, is a source of great humor on television and great sadness in real life.

In the alcoholic family, if Homer were to begin the recovery process, it would throw the whole system out of balance. When the identified sick person gets well, all of a sudden everybody has to scramble to find a new role. In extreme situations, members of the family will unconsciously or even consciously sabotage a recovering alcoholic. A known dysfunction or disease can seem more comfortable than an unknown wellness.

 ## FAMILY SCULPTING WITH ROPES AND CARABINERS

NEEDS: Gather a lot of carabiners (not necessarily climbing carabiners; you can get the key chain versions at the checkout stands of most outdoor stores). You will also need rope or string (a variety of sizes and lengths) to represent the strength of participants' connections to each of their family members.

FACILITATOR NOTE: I was first introduced to family sculpting when I began taking courses to become a chemical dependency counselor. In brief, it involves making a sculpture with people who represent the members of your family. In a typical alcoholic family it might look like this:

Mother supporting father, who has his shoulders slumped and his head down.
Hero trying to support both mother and father but struggling under the effort.
Mascot smiling, perhaps making a joke.
Scapegoat standing at some distance from the family, visibly angry.
Lost child sitting peacefully and staring into space.

PROCEDURE: Have a brave volunteer select members of the class who are willing to represent members of the volunteer's family. Have the volunteer choose the rope or string and carabiner that represent his connection to each family member. With himself at the center, the volunteer connects the ropes to each member. This creates a powerful visual effect. The ropes should vary in length to show physical or emotional distance (for example, a student might have a strong connection to his father, but the father lives in another state).

OBSERVATIONS/QUESTIONS: This can be an emotionally loaded activity. How far you take it depends on your group. I have used this as a generalized model for educational purposes and with intrepid classes, each student has done their own structure. It can also be done in small groups if participants want more privacy. Since family education is such a neglected issue in this country, many students have little baseline for "normal." You may need to emphasize that it is natural to have strong connections to some family members and weaker connections to others. You can also completely avoid the family role labels and focus only on connections.

1. Did anybody experience strong emotions during this activity?
2. Where did you feel that feeling in your body?
3. How will you use the information you have gained here?
4. Are there family members with whom you would like to have a stronger connection?
5. How do you plan to accomplish that goal?
6. Do you do things that push family members away?
7. What does your family do that makes it close?

GENOGRAM

FACILITATOR NOTE: This is an extremely emotionally loaded activity. If you are not prepared, don't do it. It is, however, a great denial buster. Make sure they are ready!! And you are too!!

PROCEDURE: First have your group members create their own family trees. I use circles for females and triangles for males. Here's the code I use:

A = ALCOHOL/DRUG PROBLEMS
B = BATTERED
Ca = CANCER
Co = CODEPENDENT
Dv = DIVORCE
Di = DIABETES

M = MENTAL ILLNESS
RA = RECOVERING ALCOHOLIC/ADDICT
Su = SUICIDE
Sm = SMOKER
T = TRAUMA TO THE FAMILY
V = COMBAT VETERAN

Inevitably there will be a child who is adopted. I take this opportunity to point out that some of these factors are genetic, such as alcoholism. Other factors, such as divorce, can be patterns. You can personalize the codes. If, for example, there is a recurring disease like Parkinson's, have them create a code for it. Other addictions might include eating disorders.

I generally follow this up with my Disease Theory of Alcoholism lecture with a focus on genetics (see page 2 in the Introduction). Depending on the audience, I may share my own genogram.

OBSERVATIONS/QUESTIONS: This activity tends to debrief itself. I'm always amazed at how many people are willing to share their genograms. Usually one brave soul will venture forth, and then there is a chain reaction. I frontload this by telling the class that while I can guarantee that I will keep their information confidential, I cannot guarantee what everybody else will do. I have had students with a lot of "As" approach me after class for more information or concerns about their own use. One student approached me a year later and told me that while it had taken a long time, the genogram had helped him to recognize his own addiction.

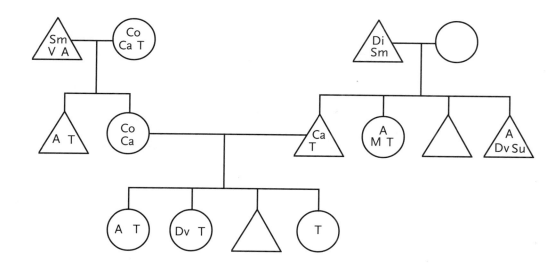

PERSONALIZED PLAYING CARDS

NEEDS: Enough drawing materials for all the participants. Deathcards (available at deathcards.com for about $5.00 a pack.) One pack is good for about 6 people.

PROCEDURE: Have the participants design their own playing card(s). The topic: Public Awareness. They can choose to make people aware of the dangers of drugs and alcohol, the effects of bullying, dropping out of school, etc. The challenge is to make the card intriguing without being inappropriate. If they need some inspiration, you might make one or two decks of the Life or Death playing cards available for them to look through or have them check out the cards online. With their permission, display the masterpieces.

OBSERVATIONS/QUESTIONS:
1. What motivated you to choose your particular topic?
2. What else could you do to educate people about this issue?
3. Of all the strategies adults use to convince kids not to smoke, what has had the most impact on you?

FACILITATOR NOTE: Media literacy is one of the most promising prevention strategies on the horizon. I like to make things relevant to the local environment. To accomplish this goal, I usually take students on an advertising tour of their town. I point out how advertisers place products and the cheap gimmicks they use to sell cigarettes to kids.

MOST PEOPLE DON'T USE DRUGS

Students can discuss people's opinions about drug use, and they will be able to see how many people at their school use drugs or alcohol. This could be a 6th or 7th grade health education activity.

NEEDS: Completed and tallied drug use survey (from ALL 6ᵗʰ and 7ᵗʰ graders). Four signs posted on different walls in the classroom—one with each of the following:
Agree
Strongly Agree
Disagree
Strongly Disagree

FACILITATOR NOTE: Have the students complete a drug use survey (see page 102) before the class period when you will do this activity. Then, tally the numbers for each category to have as statistical information to present to the class. (Note: If the results of the survey look inaccurate, use these national averages: 24.6% of eighth graders have used alcohol in the past 30 days, 8.5% have been drunk in the past 30 days.)

Write the percentages for each category on the board so students can see them when they enter the room. It's most effective to remind students that numbers such as 20% equal one in five students.

Discuss the results of the drug survey. Remind students that all/only 6ᵗʰ and 7ᵗʰ graders responded.

PROCEDURE: Explain that the following activity will help the student learn to discuss people's feelings about drug use. Point out the four signs. Explain that you will read a statement and the students will go to the sign that reflects their opinion. Tell the students that they can choose to stand under any sign, but they need to be able to explain why they chose the sign they did.

Read one of the following statements, and have students move to the sign that reflects their opinion.

People should not drink and drive.
Most people your age at this school drink alcohol frequently (at least once a month).
Smoking cigarettes will make a kid very popular.
It's cool to get drunk.
It's okay to get drunk at weddings.
I would prefer to have friends who didn't smoke marijuana.
People my age who drink know how to enjoy life more.

Read more statements and discuss them as time permits. When time is up, have the students return to their seats. Compliment them for standing up for their opinions and listening to others' opinions.

OBSERVATIONS/QUESTIONS: Discuss the statements and the students' opinions. Here are some sample questions for discussion during the activity:
1. What is your opinion of this statement? Why do you feel this way?
2. (Ask another student.) Do you agree with what that person said? Why or why not?

3. There are few people (or no one) standing under the "disagree" (or other appropriate sign). Why do you think this is the case?

4. Are you standing under the sign because it is how you really feel, or did you think that is where I wanted you to stand?

5. For those of you who agree with this statement, who remembers the actual number of people your age who drink (or smoke, etc.) at least once a month? Review the statistics if necessary to make sure it is clear that most people do not drink.

6. Do you think our school is the same as other schools regarding alcohol/tobacco/drug use? Why or why not?

7. What could you say to someone who tried to tell you that smoking/drinking/using drugs would help you fit in?

8. Look around the room at where everybody is standing. What does that tell you about the people in this class?

9. Think of your best friend. If s/he told you that it's cool to get drunk, would you agree? What would you think of your friend?

Pose the following question to the students and have them discuss it.
Suppose a new kid just moved into your neighborhood and wanted to know how you, as a class, felt about alcohol and drug use. What would you tell him/her?

Review the main points of this exercise:
- Most students do not use drugs.
- Students don't need to fall for peer pressure because they know that, in fact, most people do not use drugs.

DRUG USE SURVEY

Answer the following questions as honestly as possible.
Your answers will be tallied and used in class as part of a future lesson.

1. Have you had any alcohol to drink in the last 30 days?

    YES - just a few sips   YES - more than a few sips   NO

2. Have you smoked one or more cigarettes in the last 30 days?

    YES   NO

3. Have you smoked one or more marijuana cigarettes in the last 30 days?

    YES   NO

4. Have you been drunk or felt drunk from drinking alcohol in the last 30 days?

    YES   NO

5. Do you think you might drink at least some alcohol every month 2 years from now?

    YES   NO

6. Do you think you might try smoking cigarettes 2 years from now?

    YES   NO

7. Do you think you might try smoking marijuana 2 years from now?

    YES   NO

ALCOHOLISM BELL CURVE ACTIVITY

A common feature of ATOD education has been the addiction and recovery curve. It's often presented as a slide down followed by a rise up. It fulfills the valuable function of providing hope while still pointing out the realities. Like many otherwise staid activities, you can make it "active."

FACILITATOR NOTE: Pick several key points along the curve and have the students brainstorm solutions for ways to help. Remind them that ultimately they cannot control what another person will do. A frequent technique used by counselors is to remind children of the three Cs when it comes to another person's alcoholism. While most prevention programs focus on getting kids to refuse alcohol, tobacco, and other drugs, the painful reality is that one in eight children live with an alcoholic parent.

> They didn't CAUSE the alcoholism.
> They can't CURE the addiction.
> They can learn how to COPE.

PROCEDURE: This activity is not as exciting as some of the others, but students get a good understanding of the disease concept after they do it. To make the experience more "active," print an incident on a 3 x 5 card and have the class determine the order. For example, you might print "Promises and resolutions fail" on a card or any of the following:

Early morning drinks (wake and bake).
Onset of memory blackouts.
Obsession with drinking/using.
Daily use—obsessive drinking continues in vicious circles.
Complete defeat.
Learns alcoholism is an illness.
Stops taking alcohol.
Realistic thinking.
Regular nourishment taken.
Meets former addicts who are normal and happy.

OBSERVATIONS/QUESTIONS:
1. What could this person have done differently?
2. What could the adults in this person's life have done differently?
3. What could this person's friends have done differently?
4. If you knew that you were at high risk to develop addiction problems, how would it affect the choices you make?

VARIATIONS: You can do something similar with any "matching item" type worksheet. Copy the matching item information on 3 x 5 cards and have the class find the partner that matches their card. Remember: Make it move!

TO BE READ FROM LEFT TO RIGHT →

ADDICTION & RECOVERY

Addiction (descending path, left to right):

- OCCASIONAL RELIEF DRINKING
- CONSTANT RELIEF DRINKING COMMENCES
- ONSET OF MEMORY BLACKOUTS
- INCREASE IN ALCOHOL TOLERANCE
- SURREPTITIOUS DRINKING
- INCREASING DEPENDENCE ON ALCOHOL
- URGENCY OF FIRST DRINKS
- FEELINGS OF GUILT
- UNABLE TO DISCUSS PROBLEM
- MEMORY BLACKOUTS INCREASE
- DRINKING BOLSTERED WITH EXCUSES
- DECREASE OF ABILITY TO STOP DRINKING WHEN OTHERS DO IT
- GRANDIOSE & AGGRESSIVE BEHAVIOR
- PERSISTENT REMORSE
- EFFORTS TO CONTROL FAIL REPEATEDLY
- PROMISES & RESOLUTIONS FAIL
- TRIES GEOGRAPHICAL ESCAPES
- LOSS OF OTHER INTERESTS
- FAMILY & FRIENDS AVOIDED
- WORK & MONEY TROUBLES
- UNREASONABLE RESENTMENTS
- NEGLECT OF FOOD
- LOSS OF ORDINARY WILLPOWER
- TREMORS & EARLY MORNING DRINKS
- DECREASE IN ALCOHOL TOLERANCE
- PHYSICAL DETERIORATION
- ONSET OF LENGTHY INTOXICATIONS
- MORAL DETERIORATION
- IMPAIRED THINKING
- DRINKING WITH INFERIORS
- INDEFINABLE FEARS
- UNABLE TO INITIATE ACTION
- OBSESSION WITH DRINKING
- ALL ALIBIS EXAUSTED
- VAGUE SPIRITUAL DESIRES
- COMPLETE DEFEAT ADMITTED

CRUCIAL PHASE

CHRONIC PHASE

OBSESSIVE DRINKING CONTINUES IN VICIOUS CIRCLES

Recovery (ascending path):

- HONEST DESIRE FOR HELP
- TOLD ADDICTION CAN BE ARRESTED
- LEARNS ALCOHOLISM IS AN ILLNESS
- STOPS TAKING ALCOHOL
- MEETS FORMER ADDICTS WHO ARE NORMAL & HAPPY
- ASSISTED IN MAKING PERSONAL STOCKTAKING
- RIGHT THINKING BEGINS
- SPIRITUAL NEEDS EXAMINED
- PHYSICAL OVERHAUL BY DOCTOR
- ONSET OF NEW HOPE
- APPRECIATION OF POSSIBILITIES OF NEW WAY OF LIFE
- START OF GROUP THERAPY
- REGULAR NOURISHMENT TAKEN
- DIMINISHING FEARS OF THE UNKNOWN FUTURE
- REALISTIC THINKING
- RETURN OF SELF-ESTEEM
- NATURAL REST & SLEEP
- DESIRE TO ESCAPE GOES
- FAMILY & FRIENDS APPRECIATE EFFORTS
- ADJUSTMENT TO FAMILY NEEDS
- NEW CIRCLE OF STABLE FRIENDS
- NEW INTERESTS DEVELOP
- FACTS FACED WITH COURAGE
- REBIRTH OF IDEALS
- INCREASE OF EMOTIONAL CONTROL
- APPRECIATION OF REAL VALUES
- FIRST STEPS TOWARD ECONOMIC STABILITY
- CARE OF PERSONAL APPEARANCE
- CONFIDENCE OF EMPLOYERS
- RATIONALIZATIONS RECOGNIZED
- CONTENTMENT IN SOBRIETY
- GROUP THERAPY & MUTUAL HELP CONTINUE
- INCREASING TOLERANCE
- ENLIGHTENED & INTERESTING WAY OF LIFE OPENS UP WITH WAY AHEAD TO HIGHER LEVELS THAN EVER BEFORE

REHABILITATION

Recreated from the original version as it appeared in M. M. Glatt, "Group Therapy in Alcoholism," The British Journal of Addiction, Vol. LIX, No. 2 (January, 1958).

Changing the Message © 2004, Wood'N' Barnes Publishing & Distribution, 800-678-0621

The four characteristics of the wasicu (greedy ones) world are fear, anger, jealousy and confusion. When you see these things you will need patience, endurance, alertness, and awareness.
–Wallace Black Elk

HiGH ROPES COURSE

CREATiNG SHiFT

For years I have listened to elders talk about how tough the old people were, how they used to eat natural food, walk everywhere, and jump in icy rivers year round. I try to emulate those examples as much as possible while still living in the modern world. Last year, for reasons still slowly being revealed to me, I decided to start my own private polar bear club. Each day on the way home from work, I jumped into glacial-fed Canyon Creek or the Klickitat River. On weekends, it was Bowman Creek, which is just up the road from my house.

During September it was easy. The days were still hot, and it was quite refreshing. Changes in my attitude and perceptions about my daily dip gradually became apparent. Initially, I would pause and work up the courage to jump in. My mind would work on me a little bit. After a while, I decided to quit being silly. I had made a commitment. A life principle I follow is that when I make a commitment, whether it's publicly or privately, I follow through no matter what. October wasn't too bad until the end of the month. The creek near my house froze, and I had to work a while to break the ice before I could jump in.

At a recent conference of highly creative, adventurous types, I encouraged people to join me in my morning dip. I had no takers. These were people who facilitate and run high ropes courses for a living. This was something new, and they weren't quite ready or perhaps they just didn't want to. On the second morning, one man accompanied me just to see what it was like. He wanted to know why I felt a need to jump in. I explained commitment, and he understood that. I had to really think about the core issue. The conclusion I came to was that my daily dip was all about facing my fears. Initially, I went through the process of breaking through that fear. There are some reasonable fears. Hypothermia is an obvious concern. Fear is reasonable and expected for many environments, among them the very ones we are examining in this book, including the high elements. But if I'm going to pinpoint the most common fear for our purposes, more than anything people are afraid of temporary discomfort and pushing their limits.

As in many things that stretch us beyond perceived limits, I have received quite a few pay-offs. When the flu was raging around this winter, I experienced a few brief sniffles and it moved right through me. After a day of counseling, the icy dip seems to wash off the residue of human pain. Now I really look forward to it. It has given me a new confidence. I have stretched myself just a little. As a counselor, facilitator, and teacher I have to be willing to keep stretching. This somehow gives permission to those around me to keep stretching too.

It is not absolutely necessary to have a high ropes course to achieve a fundamental shift in your classroom and school climate. Although it is a valuable tool when available and possible, other ways to create shift include a weekend retreat, a canoe or rafting trip or creating and completing a project. I noticed that every time a class that I working with was able to get out of the building for a structured retreat of some sort, they shifted forward in their progress. (See change math on page 24.)

While we've addressed fear and commitment in the processes of becoming ourselves or guiding our students, often we must address those issues in the academic and administrative environments within which we work. Administrators and others in positions of responsibility can either confirm your fears or become your biggest advocates when trying to initiate a program like we're addressing in this book. Sometimes these fears are insurmountable, and often regulations and policies require some dismantling or restructuring. Some education might be in order. On the other side of that education, even in the struggle for "selling" your brand of "treatment," the advocate can be created and the system changed. In the process of "creating the shift" within the system, the point can be made that your students are probably safer on the high ropes course than they are on the football field, the soccer field, the basketball court, and these days, even the bus ride home. Ropes courses have a safety record that any industry would envy.

From my own experience, "finding a place" for a high elements program within a school district can be much like my first plunge into the frigid water. In fact, for 5 years, while traveling around like a circuit rider to various schools, I checked out all the gymnasiums in our rural district. I was looking for a facility that could be used year round. In addition, I was assessing the level of possible acceptance for my proposed high ropes course. One school in particular loved the idea. In addition, they had a gymnasium with huge, exposed, steel trusses. The steal trusses would provide a convenient point of attachment for climbing "elements" and belay lines. All the factors meshed so magically that I knew Klickitat was the spot. We had staff buy-in and support, administrative support, student interest, and the ideal facility. If any of these factors is missing, there is still groundwork to do.

The groundwork I did went like this:

The students and I took the PE teacher on several trips to an outdoor high ropes course in another town. The gym was his turf, and I needed to respect that. He immediately saw the value as he watched his students. Like many committed teachers, the bottom line for him was whether or not the students would benefit.

I also attended more substance abuse coalition meetings than I can remember. I even went so far as to join one. I started connecting with the people in the coalitions and the schools and in little bites introduced them to a new way of looking at prevention.

After the groundwork had been done, there was one more crucial step. I was standing in the staff room by the coffee machine thinking about how to approach the superintendent. The conversation went something like this:

"Good morning, Dr. Wild. How are you this morning?"

"Good, how are you?"

"Great; say do you have a minute?"

"Sure, I can give you 5 minutes."

"Well, Dr. Wild, I belong to several different substance abuse coalitions, and one of the things we do is sit around and evaluate the emotional intelligence of various superintendents around here, and you came out pretty high. If I could bring you a high ropes course, would you want it?"

"Yes, I think that's something I would be interested in. Let me know what we need to do."

Although you may be able to detect a little cynicism in my portrayal of the dialogue, understand that in reality, after our discussion, we were on our way. My original idea was to put a climbing wall on one end of the gym. After multiple conversations with the builder and the engineers, it became clear that idea would be cost-prohibitive. Eric Marter of Team Synergo came up with the idea of a modular system that could be suspended from the center beam in the gym. He and his crew created several "elements" that could be taken up and down with the use of the manlift. Our humble little ropes course reminds me of a giant Tinker Toy® system. Many of the parts can be mixed to create different levels of challenge, and we can add "elements" as money comes in.

It may not be the route for everyone, but it's working for us. Dream your own high ropes course, find your challenge, meet it, and who knows—maybe your mantra can be "Build it and they will come!"

In the event you make it happen, I'd like to suggest some elements for you to consider implementing. **Safety is such a monumental issue when considering the construction of a high ropes environment.** With that in mind, I only feel comfortable giving you a core amount of information about each element's physical attributes. Instead, I want to use this opportunity to share some ideas about processing the experiences of the participants. **It is imperative that you involve knowledgable and certified ropes course designers and builders in the process. In order to competently facilitate these activities you must receive advanced training from an experienced and accredited instructor.**

GIANT SWING

The Giant Swing is an unbelayed activity and provides a safe place to start. The student, who is in a climbing harness, is clipped into a cable connected to the top beam. A rope goes through a pulley, which is also connected to the center beam. That rope runs through yet another pulley connected by a ringbolt at ground level to the gym wall. On this end of the rope are the student's classmates, who will pull her up as far and as fast as she is willing to go. The student in the swing connects to the haul line by means of a quick-release system.

At no time does this system compromise the safety of the harness. A short, 3-foot rope is wrapped around and through one carabiner that is on the end of the haul line and another carabiner connected to the student's harness. When the student is ready, she releases the short rope and swings. The primary value of this activity is that the dynamics easily demonstrate the "choose your trust" concepts. The student can go as high as she wants, and she can release and swing whenever she chooses.

FACILITATOR NOTE: I cannot stress strongly enough the importance of removing any and all pressure to make any student climb or swing. Internal pressures are difficult to measure and control, but they can be addressed. Overly praising a student who makes it all the way to the top or takes multiple healthy risks can be just as damaging as exhortations to climb. In many ways, it's almost better if a student doesn't go all the way on all of the elements. It gives him/her something to work on. By the time your class is ready for the high ropes course, most students should have had a chance to stretch and grow. I stress repeatedly that nobody has to do anything that feels physically or emotionally unsafe.

Before, during, and after, I talk a lot about healthy risks, unhealthy risks, calculated risks and perceived risks. This provides a convenient backdoor to address substance abuse and other teen issues. I can make some inroads if I know a student well and have some inside information that s/he is involved in some risky behaviors.

"So you don't want to climb. That's cool. You know I wouldn't ask you to do anything you don't want to do, but I do have to ask you, is it more of a risk to climb the ladder or to get in a car with a boy who has been drinking?"

Sometimes I continue such a dialogue, and other times I quickly move on, leaving the student's mind to do the rest of the work.

CENTIPEDE

The Centipede is a series of four- to eight-foot 4" x 4" poles, hung vertically from the center beam at our place. Various synthetic climbing holds and 6-inch staples are the only means by which the student can ascend. Since the poles are all different, the challenge level can easily be shifted by changing the order of the poles. In this element the student climbs solo and is belayed from the ground.

FACILITATOR NOTE: This is a fairly straightforward climb, but there are several ways to shift the dynamics. One variation I have used is to leave off the last 4 x 4, the result being that the only way most students can access the Centipede is to ask for help. Sometimes I point this out, and other times I leave it up to them to figure out. An occasional student will struggle and struggle until s/he does not have enough strength to climb. This might be interpreted by some as "failure," and it's important to debrief this type of strategy.

OBSERVATIONS/QUESTIONS:
1. What did you need to do to start your climb?
2. Is asking for help difficult for you?
3. Are there other situations in your life where it would have been good to ask for help?
4. How do we know when to ask for help?
5. What signs should we look for?

The flipside of this strategy is that I also watch to see if students will offer help to the struggling climber.

6. How can you tell when somebody needs help?
7. Do you offer help to people when they need it?
8. What do you do when people refuse your help?
9. When is helping helpful?
10. When is helping counterproductive?

 CAVING LADDER

The Caving Ladder is assembled from thin steel tubes and steel cables. An unsteady climber can get it swinging, which adds to the challenge. Most students can climb this with relative ease, so it's a good starter element. (If you start with a difficult element that frustrates the students, they may not want to try what comes next.) Like the Centipede, this is a solo climb and is belayed from the ground. Once students have demonstrated that they can climb this, I might ask them to climb it blindfolded.

FACILITATOR NOTE: One agile young man climbed it halfway up, blindfolded, using only his hands. While this was an impressive feat, he remarked that if he had received the help of verbal directions, he could have made it all the way up. In that situation, I reinforced that everybody has different levels of trust and challenge. A young man who can easily climb everything may find it difficult, if not impossible, to cry in front of his peers. What represents more risk and courage?

After a few years of using the Caving Ladder and the Centipede separately, I tried placing them nearly side by side. When a student on either element was struggling, s/he could seek assistance from the other climber. As in other similar situations, sometimes I point this out, and sometimes I don't.

OBSERVATIONS/QUESTIONS:

1. Do we reach out to help others in this community?
2. How do we look at struggle? Do we look through compassionate eyes, or do we look on struggle with disdain?
3. What would happen if somebody was always there to reach out when we needed or asked for help?
4. Have you thought about reaching out to somebody but didn't?

FACILITATOR NOTE: An often-heard term in the chemical dependency field is "co dependency." A quick search on the Internet will turn up thousands of sites on the subject. Instead of focusing on the negative aspects of this modern malady, I try to shift people's thinking to "interdependence." When we shift the focus to everybody always looking out for everybody, we create a "hoop." If we know that everybody is looking out for us while we look out for them, we create a powerful sense of security. This sense of security provides freedom to learn and grow. When we give too much energy to a single person, this creates all sorts of confusion.

 ## GIANT'S LADDER

The Giant's Ladder consists of a series of horizontal 8-foot 4" x 4"s connected by steel cables of various lengths. The difficulty level can be easily modified by changing the cables around. With a group that needs a strong challenge, I will adjust the cables so that few if any of the 4 x 4s hang level. We have quite a few swaged cables ranging from 3 to 6 feet. I can connect the entire ladder with just 3-foot cables for younger climbers. I can also remove the bottom rungs and replace them with sections of the Centipede. What makes this element different from the other elements is that it's designed for two climbers who are belayed from the ground.

If my group is ready for the high course, then it is ready for this challenge: "Look around at who's here and think about who you have had the biggest issues with. That's your partner. A universal law of human behavior is that those who annoy us the most are the people we have the most in common with."

Another way to pick partners is to ask people to climb with somebody they would really like to get to know better. Whatever happens, I watch as they climb. Younger climbers will sometimes be oblivious to the design of the element. They might just begin climbing and ignore a person who is just a few feet away. I have also rigged this element so that they have to ask for help to get on the first rung.

When I am setting up this element, I hang a bell from the top beam and just a little to the outside so the students have to reach out quite a ways to ring it. The only rule of the bell is that they can only ring it if they both get to the top. They can go to the top by themselves, but they cannot ring the bell.

FACILITATOR NOTE: In a goal- and grade-oriented culture such as the typical school, it's not just students that need help shifting their thinking. Teachers might be heavily invested in making sure that their students get all the way to the top. This type of thinking comes from a sincere but unconscious place. One student had great difficulty getting even halfway up. A combination of fear and fatigue kept her from climbing further. Her teacher decided to climb with her to make sure she got to the top. The teacher got her there, but she short-circuited the student's process because of her own needs.

When I frontload the high ropes course, I make sure that kids get the message that it's not about getting to the top. I just ask them to go one step beyond what they're comfortable with. For some, that's just getting into a harness. Several students have similar experiences of fear. When I debrief, I make sure they get the message that there is no shame in this. Everybody learns at their own pace. A teacher who can climb anything may lack the more important skill of going directly to a person with whom he has an issue.

The entire experience with this teacher and student made me really uncomfortable. Quite a few students had not made it all the way up. As they watched this, I saw them wanting to question the process. They knew something was not quite right, but they didn't know how to question the process. It was out of step with everything else we had been doing. Before our time on the course came to an end, I had an opportunity to climb with one of my older student assistants. She needed a little help on some of the rungs, but in general, it was an easy climb. As we neared the top, I paused one rung away from being able to touch the top beam and asked my belayer to lower me down. When I got down, one of the students asked me why I didn't go all the way up. "I didn't need to," I responded.

 ## PAMPER POLE

One day you'll be lying there in your bed and you will understand everything. You'll know why you lived and what everything meant and why it happened. Then shortly afterwards, you'll croak. So don't be in a hurry to figure everything out. –Buck Ghosthorse

The Pamper Pole is the peak. It's better than any drug devised by man. Jumping toward a perhaps obtainable goal with the surety that somebody is watching for you and will catch you when you fall is the essence of common unity. Do the students and teachers see that? Some do, and some need a little debriefing to understand. Some will never understand. Some will understand years from now. One thing I have learned from hanging around spiritual teachers of various stripes is that I don't need to understand everything right now.

Like the Giant Swing, the Pamper Pole involves a lot of people. The pole itself is a 20-foot 6" x 6" treated beam with 6-inch staples and climbing holds. Four ropes go out in four different directions to support the pole. It takes at least three people per rope. The pole sits in a heavy steel bracket supported by a plywood frame. Our humble little Pamper Pole is not as high as other Pamper Poles, but no matter how carefully the people on the stabilizing ropes are, it moves.

After the climber, who is belayed from the ground, has ascended the pole and is standing carefully on top of the 6 x 6 pole, she has another task. She must try to jump and grab a trapeze bar hanging from the center beam. For younger children, we will put a rubber chicken on a pulley and a rope. Not only can we lower or raise it easily, but it also seems to shift the fear dynamic a little bit.

OBSERVATIONS/QUESTIONS:
1. What goal do you have that may require you to leap a little bit?
2. Are you doing everything you can to reach your goals?
3. What help do you need from us or from your classmates, to reach your goals/dreams?

Another way to look at the Pamper Pole is as a natural high. After the student has leapt and either caught or not caught the trapeze bar and his heart is leaping through his throat, I can point out that a natural high is always the best high. Why would we choose anything else?

COMMUNITY CONNECTION

A day on the course involves a lot of community connections. I must communicate with the gym teacher to see if the gym is being used. There are the usual permission slips and parent questions. (You will find a sample of a letter to the parents on page 122.) What makes our humble little ropes course different is how it's run. There is a true feeling of community. Because our course is on site, we have a lot more leeway. On a typical course in other school districts, the students are bussed away to some remote location. The course is run by people whom they may have met for the first time that day.

After our course was built, a few of the staff members were trained in the basics. If we are on the course for 2 to 4 hours, belayers might come and go, but the lead instructor stays. The first hour might involve the business manager belaying. The second hour might see the in-school suspension person belaying one of her frequent customers. The in-house counselor usually stops by and may do some private debriefing with a student. Perhaps a student and teacher would be climbing the Giant's Ladder together. To me, it feels like a big family. It's the closest we can get to an Amish barn raising.

The world we imagine is the world we create.
The world we create is the world we imagine.

One of my frequent partners on the high ropes course is Master Sergeant Bill Smith of the Oregon National Guard. From the outside, we look quite different. He comes to our course in full fatigues and combat boots. I arrive in my Gramicci®s and colorful shoes. His hair is closely cropped, and mine is long. When Bill's son strayed from the path several years ago, Bill pulled him from school and had him splitting wood all day long. When my son apprenticed with me in my sea kayak business and he forgot his water bottle, he went without water that day. That may seem harsh, but he survived. When Bill gets excited and well into his military mode, I might walk right up and give him a kiss on his forehead. He'll laugh and keep on moving. We probably come from different ends of the political spectrum, but we are moving toward the same goals.

About a year and a half ago, I was listening to National Public Radio when I heard an eerily familiar voice: "Clip, flip, lock, and squeeze. Screw down so you don't screw up!" It was Bill Smith, and he was running a ropes course in Israel. He had volunteered for a 1 year tour of duty in the Middle East. Somehow he had found or built a ropes course in the midst of the madness over there. Bill is passionate about the possibilities of the ropes course for changing people's lives. What really changes people's lives, however, is his passion. More than one young person I have run into looks to Bill as a father figure. We are twin sons of different mothers.

The high ropes course is rich with metaphors and figurative language. A rope becomes a "lifeline." Leaping from a simple wooden platform becomes a "leap of faith." We used to use carabiners with screw-down gates. That's where the "screw down so you don't screw up" line came from. Now that the industry is moving toward self-locking carabiners, we'll have to get some new lines. Carabiners are still "lifelinks." When a person is "on belay," s/he quite literally have your life in his/her hands. When we bring students into the institution we call "public education," we have their lives in our hands. For students who come from homes with alcoholism, drug addiction, divorce, or abuse, we are their lifelines and lifelinks. We have little power to change the immediate circumstances of their lives. We have much power to change the circumstances of their hearts and minds.

The next phase of the course is having older students run it. Legally they can do everything except for the belaying and the set up.

A DREAM?

I'm lying in the hammock in my office at the Klickitat County Adventure High School. The school has been running successfully for 10 years now. Students grow and raise their own food as part of the school's permaculture based science program. Although the school is nonprofit, it is supported by revenues from junior and senior learning projects. As part of the school's commitment to community building, a percentage of the profits support the community food co-op. Food banks have become obsolete since nobody would dream of an economic system that drives people to such desperate measures. The school is a national model for responsible capitalism. Because most of the people in the county have invested in the utility intertie direct solar, wind, and hydro systems, people don't have to choose between food and heat. The teachers remain excited because they can rotate in and out of their positions without worrying about losing their retirement. If they feel that teaching is too much for right now, they can apply to get into one the many other jobs that are available.

Austin, a senior who has attended the school since 3rd grade, bursts into my office. "The employee group from Microsoft is here."

"Is everything up?"

"Well, Lisa has to finish setting up the Vertical Jungle, but other than that we are ready to go."

"Did they do their needs assessment with the Hologram program?"

"There's two more to go."

"So what's your read on them?"

"Most of them look okay, but there's one man who looks pretty tense."

"Have you reviewed their medical forms and made sure they have all their paperwork in?"

"I did all that yesterday."

"Are there any medical concerns?"

"One woman has a titanium and plastic knee, but she says it works fine."

"Okay. Get them circled up, and I'll be right out."

Maybe that was just a dream. Maybe the idea of students running corporate retreats is a silly idea. Maybe I will be long in the ground before people can imagine and then create such possibilities. Maybe, just maybe, some oddball dreamer type who hasn't been programmed by the cubicle drones will sit in some interminably long staff meeting and ask all the wrong questions.

AFTERWORD

THE ULTIMATE INITIATIVE

Free your heart and your mind will follow.

Over time, an experienced and effective facilitator can get almost any group of people to play, to figure out how to get the bucket off the ceiling using only a box of toothpicks, and to have deep, meaningful discussions about the meaning of it all—freedom, life, love, joy, pain. Eventually, prevention specialists will figure out how to make sure that no child starts smoking. In a not-too-distant future, important people will understand that we cannot continue to just lock children up for having the disease of alcoholism and trying to escape a system that no longer meets their needs. In a free America, corporations will no longer have unlimited access to our children. Somebody important will figure out that Johnny's consumption of two to five sodas a day is linked to his inability to pay attention, his beginning to smoke, his poor academic performance, his looming addiction, and his eventual incarceration. Somebody important will figure out that feeding children is more important than living in an 8,000-square-foot house in a gated community. (I can't figure out if those people are locked in or locked out.)

The change process as people know is long-term. I have been using cell phones for about 10 years now. Only in the last 2 years have I programmed any numbers into my phone, although that service has existed for quite a long time. In the last 3 years, I began using CDs. My wife still does not use the ATM machine, nor is she interested. She prefers the little human contact that is still available in a small town where ID is still not necessary and this fact is a point of pride. Not all change helps. Not all technology helps our development as humans. As people who are interested in nurturing and helping children to learn and grow, we must continually question our own precious programs. I love the outdoors. I love playing games with people who really love to play, but I am always moving toward a goal of a better world.

When I do presentations, I have some messages that I always try to remember to communicate. The first of these is that I consider a culture which has created a need for a job such as mine to be a culture desperately in need of help. The second is that I want to work myself out of a job. (When I question the sacred cows of education, I'm probably moving toward that goal sooner than I planned on.) The third message is that ropes is the medium but not necessarily the message. There are many paths up the mountain. Theater, art, dance, music, and horticulture therapy are just a few of the ways to create a world in which children can grow and thrive.

I commonly experience similar reactions when I show up at a school where I haven't been for a while. Elementary children will run up and hug me. "Jeff's here!" will be shouted in a classroom when I try to sneak in. They also complain that they don't play the games when I'm not around because the teachers are too busy. I must be honest and admit this feeds my ego, but on a much deeper level it disturbs me. One teacher I work with has much more experience facilitating than I do, but he's there day in and day out. He also has to plan multiple lessons, deal with the inevitable soul-crushing weight of building politics, and figure out whether he can afford to work there and still feed his family. With the recent rise in insurance premiums, most teachers have experienced a net loss in pay. They must also contend with the politically driven state testing drama. When they go home, they have to listen to talk shows on both the left and right bashing the education system. No wonder everybody looks forward to my arrival with my rubber chickens and ropes.

All humanistic endeavors are eventually crushed by their own weight. –Sam Dunlap

In between all the rhetoric about the recent war and the debates of whether or not we should have pursued military solutions, I caught a common thread. The women in Afghanistan could not wait to get back to school. Having lost the freedom to learn, they valued education above many other things. Freedom of mind and spirit is perhaps the highest freedom of all. Faulty perceptions, however, dominate the human consciousness. We view the world through voluntary filters of culture, experience, belief, fears, and hopes, among other things. In many indigenous cultures and until recently, Eastern cultures, the student seeks the teacher. In modern Western culture, the teacher seeks the student and jails her if she doesn't show up enough. I don't see this paradigm shifting anytime soon. For far too many children, the perception is that school is something that happens to them. We need to create schools where children want to be. To do this we must return to the first rule of change: All change begins within.

We must embody the change we want to see. –Gandhi

I prosper from illusions that I work to defeat. The Myth of the Outside Hero pervades the consciousness of even the most advanced institutions. The Myth helps my program run. The Myth provides untold profits to legions of consultants, facilitators, and counselors. After a well-run day or week retreat or even at the end of a successful group, a wonderful feeling swirls in the breeze. The group has gelled and performed well at anything. They perceived conflicts as opportunities for learning and growth. They were curious about the thoughts, feelings, and beliefs of all members. All members rotated leadership depending on the demands of the task at hand. An infectious sense of humor dominated. When a member was having a difficult time, a groundswelling of support and empathy spontaneously arose. I hope you know and have experienced this feeling.

The quest and the challenge is to make that high degree of functionality a way of life. I don't want readers to get a sense that I am trying to create a Utopia. Highs and lows are a normal part of existence. The stages of group development do not flow in a smooth, straight line. A circle, a spiral, or perhaps even a double helix provide a more accurate model. Lessons come around repeatedly until we learn them well. When we learn one lesson, along come people who are learning the same lesson. How we help them learn defines our character. In my own life and in the lives of great people I have known, the theme of overcoming adversity weaves a common thread. In all my years of counseling and guiding, I have not been able to remove the abuse and pain that has defined the existence of some of the children I have known. All I can do is give them a glimpse and an experience of a different way. What they do with it is up to them. In many spiritual traditions, choice is understood as a sacred element of existence. When we provide a glimpse of choice, we fulfill the obligations of this life we've been given.

The field of counseling as a profession has only been around a little over 100 years. I have had my chemical dependency professional certificate for nearly 10 years. If I didn't know much about history and the history of my culture, I would think that is just how things are. My questioning mind won't let me stop there. On the back of every car I've owned for the last 10 years, I've put a bumper sticker that says "Question Authority." It sort of sticks out in a school parking lot. With my long hair, earrings, and tattoo, people often jump to the assumption that I am anti-authority. What they don't know is that I also always question my own authority. I wasn't always a sensitive, ponytail man. As I watch the growth of counseling as a profession and the proliferation of prescription drugs and their accompanying disorders, I cannot help but feel that we have gotten way off track somewhere.

I believe we create our own reality through the structures of our culture. Structures create behaviors. A little over 500 years ago in this land called Turtle Island, we had no prisons, no alcoholism, no designer drugs, no methamphetamines, and no Prozac®. We had tobacco, but in its pure form it was a medicine and it was used in prayer. This is not to say we were without problems, but we did have more successful ways of dealing with those problems. In traditional village life, whether it was Native American, Irish, or Chinese, people created relationships that met multiple needs. The idea of a single person listening to everybody's problems all day would have seemed absurd. Different people gravitated toward each other based upon mutual respect and understanding. Grandfathers, grandmothers, aunts, and uncles provided guidance and open ears for young people seeking guidance. In well-functioning villages, leaders became recognized because they were constantly looking out for the welfare of all. A leader who failed to make sure that the children were fed quickly ceased to become a leader. When hard times came, everybody suffered and survived together. This did not happen because of strict laws or coercion. It happened because it made sense.

Listening to the radio this morning I heard about some new initiative to get every kid a laptop computer. I thought about starting my own initiative to get every kid a mud pie, whoopie cushion, and rubberband shooter. "A SUPERBALL IN EVERY DESK!" would be my campaign promise.

If you can dream it, we can do it. –Sam Fast Buffalo Horse

Now for you activity skimmers, here is the Ultimate Initiative Problem. Create structures that support families. A healthy family is still the best prevention program we have. Create a classroom with your children where they want to come. Create a classroom and school where the teachers and students laugh at and learn from their mistakes. Create a community like the one I grew up in, where moms will rat you out when you're doing things you're not supposed to be doing. Create a world where children delight in leaving flowers on the doorsteps of elders without their knowledge. Create a community where all children are safe, where all children can knock on just about any door and receive welcomes and love and food. Create a world where the color of a child's skin is of no more importance than the color of her eyes. Create a common unity where children eat wholesome food, drink clean water, breathe clean air. Become somebody that children want to be like when they grow up. Create a classroom where children are excited about learning, where nobody wants to skip or be sick, because they know they will miss something fun for sure. I'll be back to check on your progress.

You can learn more about a person in an hour of play than in a lifetime of conversation. –Plato

WHAT'S IN JEFF'S BAG

- [ ] Thirty spot markers
- [ ] Fifteen fleece balls
- [ ] Fifteen stuffed sheep
- [ ] Twenty 6-foot webbing circles
- [ ] Five Rubber Chickens
- [ ] One Rubber Pig
- [ ] Chiji Processing Cards®
- [ ] Chiji Yin Yang Cards®
- [ ] Body Parts Processing Bag from Training Wheels®
- [ ] Small processing pack from Training Wheels®
- [ ] Multiple lengths and colors of webbing: two at 75 feet, four at 20 feet, one at 50 feet
- [ ] One retired climbing rope cut into three 30-foot sections and one 60-foot section
- [ ] Assorted carabiners (not necessarily for climbing)
- [ ] Four Potato Heads® and one accessory kit
- [ ] Foam Dominoes from Training Wheels®
- [ ] Four Barrel of Monkeys® barrels
- [ ] Forty-plus bandanas
- [ ] Assorted soft throwables
- [ ] Two 3 x 4 puzzles
- [ ] Feelings Cards®
- [ ] Storyline book cut and laminated
- [ ] One breakdown 6' x 10' spiderweb
- [ ] One tabletop spiderweb
- [ ] One 8' x 10' nylon tarp
- [ ] One small 8-foot parachute
- [ ] One large 24-foot parachute
- [ ] Twelve 1 1/2-inch dowels for human ladder
- [ ] Bag of clothespins

- [ ] Forty foam noodles
- [ ] Two large bags of cut-up noodles
- [ ] Six ricochet balls
- [ ] Four bouncing eggs
- [ ] Four wacky balls
- [ ] Two inflatable koosh balls
- [ ] Twenty-five blindfolds
- [ ] Twenty breakdown Hula Hoops®
- [ ] Thirty feet of 1" multiline swing rope
- [ ] Ten assorted footbags
- [ ] Forty mousetraps
- [ ] Construction survey string (on spool)
- [ ] Forty floppy Frisbees®

TEACHING TOOLS & RESOURCES

SOME DEFINITIONS AND EXAMPLES

Belay: A means of securing a climber by use of a rope, and usually a belay device, in order to prevent or minimize a fall. A **belayer** is the person on the ground or at the belay station who secures the climber.

Clove hitch:

Double barrel or fisherman's knot:

Girth hitch:

Overhand knot:

Spotter: Somebody whose job is to stand by and guard against injury during a sports event, e.g., in gymnastics. (Encarta World English Dictionary, 1999 ©Bloomsbury Publishing Plc)

Spotting: Actively protecting the progress of another participant. The spotter's main purpose is to help prevent falls causing injury. The spotter's job is not to prevent a fall, it is to prevent injury. So, if both the spotter and participant end up on the ground without serious harm, the spotter has done his job. (Chris Cavert, Affordable Portables ©1999)

Spotting position: Feet are shoulder width apart. One foot is forward and one is back. Elbows are bent with hands up in front of your body. Palms are facing outward and fingers pointing upward.

Throwable: I use 4-inch fleece balls (among other things), which are available in most PE catalogs. A good throwable does not hurt upon impact but can be felt when it hits you. It can also be lobbed a considerable distance with some degree of accuracy.

Water knot:

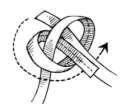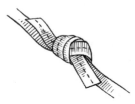

Webbing: A flat strip of very strong nylon that comes in various widths. Tubular webbing is the strongest.

Webbing circle: (also referred to as a webbing loop) Webbing that is tied in a loop to create a circle, sling, etc.

HOW PARENTS CAN HELP THEIR CHILDREN INTEGRATE LESSONS FROM THE ROPES COURSE

Dear Parents/Guardians,

In the next few weeks, we will be doing ropes course activities with students at Klickitat. Ropes courses are used in a variety of ways as a tool for building self-confidence, teaching healthy communication, and strengthening relationships.

As a Prevention Specialist, I focus on the concepts of risk.

1) Healthy Risks
2) Unhealthy Risks
3) Perceived Risks
4) Calculated Risks

These are loose categories by design. Some issues are obvious. Smoking for example is clearly an unhealthy risk. High Ropes courses have traditionally focused on Perceived Risks. The "elements" on the course are perceived to be risky but in reality they are safer than traditional sports. The talk of risk leads into concepts about challenges and or barriers:

1) Paper Walls—easily moved
2) Cubicles—a little more solid but still easy to deal with
3) Framed Walls—like the walls in many houses, moving is possible but more difficult
4) Brick Walls—can be moved but require even more effort
5) Immovable Objects—mountains, etc.

Most barriers with people are generally in their minds and can be changed or moved. I ask the children to stretch and challenge themselves in some way. For example, if a person is often talkative, I might ask them to be quiet more often. If a person is generally quiet, I might ask them to be more verbal. It is important to note that no one is required to do anything that to them represents too much of a physical or emotional risk. If you have additional questions or can come in when your child is on the course, please feel free to contact me at any time.

CLASSROOM EQ (EMOTIONAL QUOTIENT) TEST

I designed this test as a way to roughly measure the emotional intelligence in a class. It can be used as part of a staff presentation when you are trying to convince people to support your program, or you can reframe it and have students answer the questions. It serves as a quick needs assessment and can give you a solid starting point.

CLASSROOM EQ (EMOTIONAL QUOTIENT) TEST

The questions below represent two extremes of different areas and are quite generalized. Imagine a continuum from a to z. Place your classroom where you feel it fits. To further challenge yourself, come up with one or more descriptive words that match the letter you have chosen for each category. This questionnaire is designed to spur thought about the emotional quotient in your classroom.

1) SOCIAL STRUCTURE

a) Students in my classroom understand that different people have different skills and will utilize a variety of leaders depending on the situation.

b c d e f g h i j k l m n o p q r s t u v w x y

z) There are established heirarchies and roles in my classroom that are almost inescapable.

DESCRIPTIVE WORD(S):

2) SOCIAL CONSCIOUSNESS

a) Students in my classroom easily adapt to people from cultures other than their own and readily accept those they see as different from themselves and their peer group.

b c d e f g h i j k l m n o p q r s t u v w x y

z) I frequently hear degrading comments from some of my students about people who are perceived as different than themselves and their peer group.

DESCRIPTIVE WORD(S):

3) EMOTIONAL SAFETY

a) Students in my classroom treat each other with a great deal of respect.

b c d e f g h i j k l m n o p q r s t u v w x y

z) Put downs and blaming/shaming comments are frequently heard in my classroom.

DESCRIPTIVE WORD(S):

4) PHYSICAL SAFETY

a) Students in my classroom feel safe during the school day.

b c d e f g h i j k l m n o p q r s t u v w x y

z) Students in my classroom often fear for their physical safety during the school day.

DESCRIPTIVE WORD(S):

5) LATERAL THINKING

a) Students in my classroom approach complex problems with enthusiasm.

b c d e f g h i j k l m n o p q r s t u v w x y

z) Students in my classroom often seem baffled by complex problems.

DESCRIPTIVE WORD(S):

6) CONFLICT RESOLUTION

a) Students in my classroom are well versed in conflict resolution skills.

b c d e f g h i j k l m n o p q r s t u v w x y

z) Students in my classroom approach conflicts defensively and with hostility. Conflicts are rarely solved successfully.

DESCRIPTIVE WORD(S):

7) COMMUNICATION SKILLS

a) Students in my classroom are skilled communicators.

b c d e f g h i j k l m n o p q r s t u v w x y

z) Students in my classroom have great difficulty communicating with their peers.

DESCRIPTIVE WORD(S):

8) MY PERSONAL BELIEF STRUCTURE

a) I believe that thoughtfully chosen programs which are carefully implemented can positively impact the social structure of my classroom.

b c d e f g h i j k l m n o p q r s t u v w x y

z) I believe there is little I can do to change the emotional quotient of my classroom.

DESCRIPTIVE WORD(S):

QUALITIES OF HEALTHY FAMILIES

- Family members can express feelings, needs, and concerns without fear of reprisal. Expression of feelings is valued and encouraged.

- Each member is seen as valuable and integral to the family unit. Family members support each other in both divergent and convergent goals.

- Leadership is shared by both parents. Rules are consistent and reasonable. Parents explain the reasons behind rules. Mistakes are seen as a way to grow and learn. In special situations, rules can bend.

- When a problem arises, the family deals with it directly and works together to solve it. The needs of all parties are considered, but it is recognized that not all solutions meet all needs.

- The family shares common values such as respect for oneself and others, right and wrong, and spiritual practices.

- Directness, clarity, and honesty are considered to be the foundation for communication. Actions and words are congruent. All members contribute and listen.

Changing the Message © 2004, Wood'N' Barnes Publishing & Distribution, 800-678-0621

ACTIVITY LOG

I've been running these activities for nearly 20 years so I do most of my planning in my head. I have trained my mind to remember a lot of activities and typical outcomes. If you are just starting out, this log may help.

ACTIVITY: _____ AGE GROUP: _____

ACTIVITY TYPE:
Ice Breaker
Cooperative
Trust
Initiative
High Ropes

INTENDED GOAL OR OUTCOME:

ACTUAL GOAL OR OUTCOME:

FRONTLOADING/FRAMING OR FANTASY SCENARIOS:

DEBRIEFING TOPICS AND ISSUES THAT AROSE:

WHAT TO KEEP FOR NEXT TIME:

WHAT TO CHANGE NEXT TIME:

CHANGINGMESSAGE

ORGANIZATION CONTACT INFORMATION

1) HEALTH ORGANIZATIONS

The American Lung Association
61 Broadway, 6th Floor, New York, NY 10006
212-315-8700

National Diabetes Information Clearinghouse
1 Information Way, Bethesda, MD 20892-3560
1-800-860-8747 or 301-654-3327 fax 301-907-8906
e-mail: ndic@info.niddk.nih.gov

American Diabetes Association
ATTN: National Call Center
1701 North Beauregard Street, Alexandria, VA 22311

Physicians for Social Responsibility
1875 Connecticut Avenue, NW, Suite 1012, Washington, DC, 20009
202-667-4260 fax 202-667-4201
e-mail: psrnatl@psr.org

ESR National Center/Educators for Social Responsibility
23 Garden St., Cambridge, MA 02138
617-492-1764 fax 617-864-5164
e-mail: educators@esrnational.org
www.esrnational.org

2) EQUIPMENT AND ROPES COURSE BUILDERS

Challenge Masters, Inc.
821 Dock St., Box 1-16, Tacoma, WA 98402
253-279-0052 800-673-0911 fax 253-759-7548
e-mail: info@challengemasters.com
A provider of high quality, portable low ropes kits.

Mobile Team Challenge
3247 E. Lamar Alexander Parkway, Maryville, TN 37804
888-681-0146 fax 865-982-7721
e-mail: info@MobileTeamChallenge.com
Mobile Team Challenge portable ropes courses
Another provider of high quality portable low ropes kits.

Project Adventure
Corporate Office
701 Cabot Street, Beverly, MA 01915
978-524-4500 fax 978-524-4501
SOUTHEAST
P.O. Box 2447, Covington, GA 30015
770-784-9310 fax 770-787-7764
e-mail: info@pa.org
Project Adventure provides high and low ropes course construction, portable low ropes kits, trainings and a lot of great books.

National 4-H Headquarters
Families, 4-H & Nutrition
CSREES/USDA
1400 Independence Ave. SW
Washington DC 20250-2225
4-H is no longer just about agriculture. It has been a leader in providing all manner of ropes course experiences. Contact your local office for more info.

Roger Greenaway
Reviewing Skills Training
9 Drummond Place Lane
STIRLING FK8 2JF SCOTLAND
tel/fax - UK office hours (GMT)
+44 (0)1786 450968
e-mail: roger@reviewing.co.uk
This is absolutely the best Web site for a ton of ideas on debriefing experiential activities.

Training Wheels
Portable Team Building Programs and Equipment
7095 S. Garrison St., Littleton, CO 80128
888-553-0147 fax 888-553-0146
e-mail: info@training-wheels.com
Training wheels is your best source for processing debriefing materials. They also supply props for low, portable challenge activities.

Fundoing with Chris Cavert
Flagstaff, AZ
928-526-6386
www.fundoing.com
email chris@fundoing.com
Chris is an adventure based activity training and resource provider.

Erik Marter
Synergo
7266 SW 26th Ave, Portland, OR 97219
503-452-9451 fax 503-452-1521
www.teamsynergo.com
Erik and company provide great low and high ropes training. He is also an innovative, leading edge, high and low ropes course builder.

Cultivating Connections/Branch Out (Molly Foote)
907 Harris Avenue, Suite 301, Bellingham, WA 98225
e-mail: branchout@cultivatingconnections.com
Molly puts together a nice package of experiential activities that work well in a classroom environment.

Foam Noodles Resources:
Adventure Hardware 800-706-0064 (Matt McCoy)
Learned Enterprises 800-462-0411
Grip-It Adventures 877-510-2084
Life Like Products 410-889-1023 (Bob Botti)
Sport Supply Group (http://www.sportsupply.com) 800-387-3847 (ask for U.S. Distributor that
          serves your local area) - has "Big Boss" or 4" Noodles.
Gladon Co. - East Coast Distributor for Tundra Foam 800-448-6070
Prices vary; be sure to ask if the noodles are the "cut" or "un-cut" versions!

3) COOL WEBSITES

http://come-over.to/fas/videowebcast.htm
A series of free Fetal Alcohol Syndrom videos produced by national FAS trainer and good friend
Carolyn Hartness.

http://faculty.washington.edu/chudler/outside.html
Neuroscience for kids that includes a lot of interactive games that teach about the brain.

http://www.youthwork.com/activitiesinit.html
A great Web site with a lot of kid generated activities, resources and valuable links.

http://www.actsofkindness.org/
Random Acts of Kindness home page.

http://www.geocities.com/dr_adventure/activitypage.html
Christian Itin's activity page with hundreds of free activities.

Media Literacy Clearinghouse
www.med.sc.edu/medialit

http://www.nedpord.com/Niall_stuff/intelligence_test.html
Filter through the editorials, and you can take a free Multiple Intelligence test online.

http://outrageavenue.com/flash.html
A hip anti-smoking Web site that is very kid-friendly.

Mid-Continent Research for Education and Learning
2550 South Parker Road, Suite 500, Aurora, CO 80014
303-337-0990
http://www.mcrel.org
MCREL is a wonderful source of education standards and materials. They have a lot of free stuff
on their Web site.

http://www.alfiekohn.org
Alfie is one of the leading voices in education today.

P2550 South Parker Road
www.come-over.to/FAS/videowebcast.htm337-3005

http://www.tribes.com
TRIBES has a groovy Web site.

PE Central
PO Box 10262, Blacksburg, VA 24062
540-953-1043 (Mark Manross, Executive Director) fax 800-783-8124 (USA)
e-mail: pec@pecentral.org
A good source of lesson plans, ideas and equipment.

Southern Poverty Law Center
400 Washington Avenue, Montgomery, AL 36104
http://www.splcenter.org
The USA's leading civil rights organization. They publish a free magazine called *Teaching Tolerance* and distribute free videos and other publications. Quality is superb.

Play for Peace®
4750 North Sheridan Road, Suite 225, Chicago, IL 60640,
773-275-0077 fax 773-275-3385
email: info@playforpeace.org
http://www.playforpeace.org

4) RECOVERY ORGANIZATIONS

Nicotine Anonymous World Services
419 Main Street, PMB# 370, Huntington Beach, CA 92648
415-750-0328
e-mail: info@nicotine-anonymous.org

ALCOHOLICS ANONYMOUS
Grand Central Station, PO Box 459, New York NY, 10163
http://www.alcoholics-anonymous.org

National Association for Children of Alcoholics
11426 Rockville Pike, Suite 100, Rockville, Maryland 20852
888-55-4COAS 301-468-0985 fax 301-468-0987
e-mail: nacoa@nacoa.org
http://www.nacoa.org

Adult Children of Alcoholics
ACA WSO
P.O. Box 3216, Torrance CA 90510 USA
310-534-1815
e-mail: meetinginfo@adultchildren.org or info@adultchildren.org
Use for information on locating meetings.
http://www.adultchildren.org

John Bradshaw
www.johnbradshaw.com
www. creativegrowth.com
800-6-BRADSHAW

Claudia Black
www.claudiablack.com
www.themeadows.org

5) PROFESSIONAL ORGANIZATIONS

Association for Challenge Course Technology
ACCT Office
P.O. Box 255, Martin, MI 49070-0255
269-685-0670 fax 269-685-6350

Association for Experiential Education
2305 Canyon Boulevard, Suite 100, Boulder, CO 80302-5651
303-440-8844 fax 303-440-9581

National Student Assistance Association
4200 Wisconsin Avenue, NW, Suite 106-118, Washington, DC 20016
800-257-6310 fax 215-257-6997
e-mail: info@nasap.org

6) MEDIA LITERACY ORGANIZATIONS

Adbusters
1243 West 7th Avenue, Vancouver, BC, V6H 1B7 Canada
800-663-1243 worldwide, 604-736-9401 fax 604-737-6021
Adbusters is an edgy organization that is probably the leading media literacy group out there today.

Center for Media Literacy
3101 Ocean Park Boulevard, #200, Santa Monica, CA 90405
310-581-0260 fax 310-581-0270
http://www.medialit.org

New Mexico Media Literacy Project
6400 Wyoming Blvd. NE, Albuquerque, NM 87109
505-828-3129 fax 505-828-3142
e-mail: nmmlp@nmmlp.org
www.nmmlp.org

7) GOVERNMENT AGENCIES

Liz Wilhelm
The Washington State Alcohol/Drug Clearinghouse, 6535 5th Place South, Seattle, WA 98108
800-662-9111 206-725-9696 fax 206-760-0589
clearinghouse@adhl.org

SAMHSA Offices
Substance Abuse and Mental Health Services Administration
Rm 12-105 Parklawn Building 5600 Fishers Lane, Rockville, MD 20857
301-443-5700
http://www.samhsa.gov

Center for Substance Abuse Prevention Offices
> Western Region
> University of Nevada, Reno, 1664 North Virginia Street, Reno, NV 89557
> 888-734-7476 775-784-1174 fax 775-784-1840
> http://www.westcapt.org
>
> Border Region
> Arizona-Mexico Border Health Foundation, 3365 N. Campbell Ave., Ste 141, Tucson, AZ 85719
> 800-864-9260 520-887-0433 fax 520-887-0432
> e-mail: bordercapt@ambhf.org
>
> Southwest Region
> Southwest Prevention Center, University of Oklahoma, 555 Constitution Street, Ste. 132,
> Norman, OK 73072
> 800-853-2572 405-325-1454 fax 405-325-7092
> http://www.swcapt.org
>
> Central Region
> Minnesota Institute of Public Health, 2720 Highway 10, Mounds View, MN 55112
> 800-782-1878 763-427-5310 fax 763-427-7841
> http://www.ccapt.org
>
> Southeast Region
> Developing Resources for Education in America, Inc. (DREAM)
> 310 Airport Rd., Ste. D, Jackson, MS 39208
> 800-233-7326 601-933-9199 fax 601-933-1138
> http://www.secapt.org
>
> Northeast Region
> Educational Development Center, Inc., 55 Chapel Street, Newton, MA 02158-1060
> 888-EDC-CAPT 617-969-7100 fax 617-244-3436
> http://www.csapnortheastcapt.org

National Institute on Drug Abuse
National Institutes of Health
6001 Executive Boulevard, Room 5213, Bethesda, MD 20892-9561
http://www.drugabuse.gov/NIDAHome.html

NIDA and CSAP provide a lot of research on Risk and Protective Factors.

8) EXPERIENTIAL LEARNING RESOURCES

National 4-H Headquarters
Families, 4-H & Nutrition
CSREES/USDA
1400 Independence Ave. SW
Washington DC 20250-2225

Roger Greenaway
Reviewing Skills Training
9 Drummond Place Lane
STIRLING FK8 2JF SCOTLAND
tel/fax - UK office hours (GMT)
+44 (0)1786 450968
e-mail (any time!) roger@reviewing.co.uk

CHRISTIAN ITIN
Greater Rochester Collaborative MSW Program
SUNY Metro Center, 6th Floor, 228 East Main Street, Rochester, NY 14604
716-327-7453   fax 716-232-8603
e-mail: dr_adventure@go.com

9) CONSULTANTS AND RESEARCH ORGANIZATIONS

CHOICES (Creating Healthy Options In Confronting Exploitive Sexuality) of Oregon® and Steven
E. Mussack, Ph.D., Program Director
1234 High St., Suite B, Eugene, OR 97401
541-343-7643
e-mail mussack@choicesoforegon.com
PC info on thinking errors.

Jim Rough & Associates, Inc.
1040 Taylor Street, Port Townsend, WA 98368
360-385-7118 fax 360-385-6216
e-mail seminars@ToBe.net
http://www.tobe.net
Jim may belong with the great websites. He has some enlightening articles online about the
Wisdom Council.

Search Institute
The Banks Building
615 First Avenue NE, Suite 125, Minneapolis MN 55413
612-376-8955 800-888-7828
http://www.search-institute.org/
The Search Institute is the source of the 40 Developmental Assets.

Cain, Jim & Jolliff, B. (1998) *Teamwork and teamplay*. Dubuque, IA: Kendall Hunt Publishing.

Cain, Jim & Smith, Tom (2002). *The book on raccoon circles.* Tulsa, OK: Learning Unlimited

Cavert, Chirs (1999). *Affordable portables: A working book of initiative activities and problem solving elements.* Oklahoma City, OK: Wood 'N' Barnes Publishing and Distribution.

Cavert, Chris (1997). *50 ways to use your noodle*. Tulsa, OK: Learning Unlimited.

Frank, Laurie (2004). *Journey toward the caring classroom: Using adventure to create community in the classroom and beyond*. Oklahoma City, OK: Wood 'N' Barnes Publishing and Distribution.

Fluegelman, Andrew (1976). *The new games book*. Garden City, NY: Doubleday and Company.

Henton, Mary (1996). *Adventure in the classroom*. Dubuque, IA: Kendall Hunt Publishing.

Kohn, Alfie (1992). *No contest*. New York, NY: Houghton Mifflin.

Kohn, Alfie (1993). *Punished by rewards*. New York, NY: Houghton Mifflin.

Kolb, D.A. (1984). *Experiential learning: experience as the source of learning and development.* Englewood Cliffs, New Jersey: Prentice-Hall.

Kreidler, William J. & Furlong, Linda (1996). *Adventures in peacemaking: A conflict resolution activity guide.* Cambridge, MA: Educators for Social Responsibility.

LeFevre, Dale N (1988). *New games for the whole family.* New York, NY: Penguin Putnam Inc.

Luckner, John L. & Nadler, R. S. (1997). *Processing the experience: Strategies to enhance and generalize learning* (2nd ed.). Dubuque, IA: Kendall Hunt Publishing.

MacKenzie, Gordon (1998). *Orbiting the giant hairball*. New York, NY: Viking Penguin.

Rohnke, Karl (1994). *The bottomless bag again*. Dubuque, IA: Kendall Hunt Publishing.

Rohnke, Karl (1989). *Cowstails and cobras II*. Dubuque, IA: Kendall Hunt Publishing.

Rohnke, Karl (1996). *Funn stuff 1*. Dubuque, IA: Kendall Hunt Publishing.

Rohnke, Karl (1996). *Funn stuff 2*. Dubuque, IA: Kendall Hunt Publishing.

Rohnke, Karl (1998) *Funn stuff 3*. Dubuque, IA: Kendall Hunt Publishing.

Rohnke, Karl (1984). *Silver bullets*. Dubuque, IA: Kendall Hunt Publishing.

Rohnke, Karl & Butler, Steve (1995). *Quicksilver*. Dubuque, IA: Kendall Hunt Publishing.

Sakofs, Mitchell & Armstrong, George P. (2000). *Into the classroom*. Dubuque, IA: Kendall Hunt Publishing.

Scholtes, Peter R. (1988). *The team handbook: How to use teams to improve quality*. Brian L. Joiner (contributor). Madison, WI: Joiner.

Senge, Peter (2000). *Schools that learn*. New York, NY: Doubleday.

Schoel, Prouty, Radcliffe (1988). *Islands of healing: A guide to adventure based counseling*. Hamilton, MA: Project Adventure, Inc.

Sikes Sam (1998). *Executive marbles*. Tulsa, OK: Learning Unlimited.

Sikes Sam (1995). *Feeding the zircon gorilla*. Tulsa, OK: Learning Unlimited.

ABOUT THE AUTHOR

Jeff Albin is the son, grandson, and nephew of farmers, warriors, and proud matrons. He is proud of the fact that like many Americans his ancestors come from many parts of the globe. He takes much of his inspiration from the First Peoples of this continent and has spent the last fourteen years hanging out (he avoids the word studying) with Lakota spiritual teachers and elders. He credits his unique view of counseling, family, education, learning and community to the teachings of these elders, the most respected of whom is Buck Ghosthorse. Jeff believes that the solutions to our future lie in wisdom from the past. He has dedicated his life to a world where all children know true freedom and joy.

Jeff grew up in the Eastern Washington town of Wenatchee. Hunting and camping trips with his family and friends around the Great Pacific Northwest helped develop his love of nature and adventure. Much of his life has been invested in sea kayaking, rafting and as a crosscountry ski guide. In 1984, he soloed the Inside Passage in a kayak. In 1989, he co-led the first joint Russian/American sea kayak expedition down the Syr Darya river in Soviet Central Asia (Uzbekistan/Kazakhstan)). Jeff has been working in schools since 1995 as an Intervention and Prevention Specialist. His unconventional but systemic approach to prevention has earned him well deserved accolades.

Jeff facilitates corporate retreats, peer helper trainings, community building "family nights," culture camps, and is a frequently requested presenter at conferences.

He graduated from Western Washington University in 1986 with two BA's in English, one BA in Secondary Education, and a secondary teaching certificate. Following graduation, Jeff worked in social services, mental health, juvenile rehabilitation and education. He is a certified chemical dependency professional and has been working in the field since 1988 when he began running sea kayaking retreats for at-risk youth and adults in early recovery. He presently lives with his wife of 12 years off the grid in a solar and wind powered home a mile from where the county road turns to gravel.

You can contact Jeff at:

Second Wind Enterprises
PO Box 1420
Goldendale, WA 98620
Skydog@counsellor.com
509-261-0275